SEURAT

Seurat

by ALEXANDRIAN

11

CROWN PUBLISHERS, INC. - NEW YORK

Title page: Maximilien Luce
PORTRAIT OF SEURAT PAINTING, 1890
Lithograph in black and white
Bibliothèque Nationale, Paris
(SPADEM, Paris)

Translated from the French by:
ALICE SACHS

Collection published under the direction of:
MADELEINE LEDIVELEC-GLOECKNER

PHOTOGRAPHS

Clichés Musées Nationaux, Paris – A. C. Cooper, London – André Held, Ecublens, Switzerland – Jacqueline Hyde, Paris – S. Lazarus and R. Mates, New York – Otto E. Nelson, New York – John Schiff, New York – Robert Wallace, Indianapolis – John Webb, London.

Library of Congress Cataloging in Publication Data
Alexandrian, Sarane.
 Georges Seurat.

 1. Seurat, Georges Pierre, 1859–1891. 2. Artists
— France — Biography.
N6853.S48A72 759.4 [B] 79–24180
ISBN 0–517–54106–8

PRINTED IN ITALY – INDUSTRIE GRAFICHE CATTANEO S.P.A., BERGAMO – © 1980 BONFINI PRESS CORPORATION, NAEFELS, SWITZERLAND
ALL RIGHTS IN THE U.S.A. RESERVED BY CROWN PUBLISHERS, INC., NEW YORK, NEW YORK

PEASANTS DRIVING STAKES, c. 1881. Oil on panel, 5¾″ × 9½″ (14.5 × 24 cm)
Private Collection

Seurat's work as well as his personality have been subjected to misunderstanding about which he himself complained during his lifetime, and which irritated him all the more because those responsible were his admirers, who attributed to him intentions inconsistent with his temperament. At first there was a tendency to consider him a painter of poeticized reality, because his drawings evoked the atmosphere of a nocturnal fairyland, and his canvases, with their formal figures, their light strokes that formed a mosaic of multicolored dots, radiated a hieratic charm.

The exponents of this opinion were the Symbolist writers, particularly Gustave Kahn, pioneer of free verse in «Les Palais nomades» (1886), who argued that the «theory of constrast» in Neo-Impressionist art was the aesthetic equivalent of the «theory of discontinuity» in decadent poetry, and declared: «Confronted by pictorial conventions, Seurat suffered deeply from somewhat the same anguish that afflicted Mallarmé when he faced the structure of a book and the succession of pages.» Moreover, Jules Christophe, Seurat's first biographer, described him as a «Wagnerian colorist,» so that the artist worriedly asked those close to him to let him know in what way he

*Portrait of Edmond-François Aman-Jean, 1882–83. Conté crayon, 24½" × 18¾" (62.3 × 47.6 cm)
The Metropolitan Museum of Art, New York. Bequest of Stephen C. Clark*

resembled Mallarmé or Wagner. He believed himself to be solely the creator of an «optical formula» that presented a solution to a problem that had concerned Watteau and Delacroix. Even Lucie Cousturier, herself a Neo-Impressionist, said in the work she published on her master: «Seurat's procedure is that of a poet.»

Subsequently the Surrealists seconded this judgment: in 1938, in «Minotaure,» Dr. Pierre Mabille compared Seurat's drawings with the hallucinations of a waking dreamer who, his eyes misty with «the dew of dreams,» discovered a universe in which «phantoms' fluidity is crystallized». Later, André Breton paid homage to «the mind of Seurat (ever turned inward),» and numbered *Le Chahut* * among the achievements of a magical art that had the power to charm and to fascinate. Personally, I too have included Seurat among the precursors of Surrealism, to a lesser degree than Gustave Moreau, in my book, «Surrealist Art»; but I am of the opinion that, in spite of his involuntarily dream-like visions, his true importance lay in his paving the way for Cubism, for Abstractionism drawn from nature, for the visual experimentation of the Bauhaus. Seurat was the inventor of Chromo-Luminarism, and the person who introduced into painting the experimental method that Claude Bernard initiated in science; it is appropriate to study him exclusively in this connection, even at the risk of estimating if he sometimes overshot his goal.

The family to which Seurat was born, on December 2, 1959 in Paris, held nothing particularly promising for the flowering of an artistic career. His father, Antoine Seurat, a long-time bailiff at La Villette, was, in everyone's opinion, a strange character: tyrannical, demanding to be addressed as the «Honorable Officer of the Administration,» pious to the point of bigotry, he had decorated the walls of his apartment with religious pictures cut out from the publications of Epinal. ** He saw his wife and children only once a week, and the rest of the time lived alone in Raincy, where he tended the flowers in his garden; on Sundays, he celebrated mass in the basement of his house, flanked by his gardener who acted as choir boy. Paul Signac gave a curious portrait of him that he related to Félix Fénéon: «I frequently dined with him on Tuesdays, the day that this husband devoted to his marital obligations, at the home of Madame Seurat, in the company of Georges. You may also know that he was equipped with a mechanical arm — not since birth, although he had a bizarre enough personality to have sanctioned such originality — but as a result, I believe, of a hunting accident. At the table he screwed to the end of this arm knives and forks, which enabled him to cut with speed and even fury legs of lamb, fillets, chicken and game. He actually juggled with these sharp and pointed weapons, and when I sat next to him, I worried a great deal about what might happen to my eyes. Georges paid no attention to these cabaret turns.» Seurat's mother, a gentle and meek bourgeoise, took no initiative except when so ordered by this maniac.

Before Georges' birth, his parents had had a son in 1846 and a daughter in 1847, with whom he had little in common. He deplored the superficial character of his brother, Emile Seurat, a playwright whose total output consisted of two one-act comedies: «The Terrible Berniquet» (produced in 1885 at the Cluny Theatre), and «The Dentist If You Please» (a sketch for the Palais-Royal). «He liked to have stylish clothes,» he commented repeatedly. His sister, Marie-Berthe, was such a stranger to him that his closest friend did not even know that she existed; yet when she became the wife of the master glass maker Léon Appert, he presented the couple with several of his works. During his childhood, Georges enjoyed visiting his uncle, Paul Haumonté-Faivre, who had a dry goods store, «Au Père de Famille» (The Family Man), at 48, avenue des Ternes; an amateur painter, he took the boy along when he went to the outskirts of Paris to paint landscapes.

Even before he had finished his secondary school studies, Seurat took courses at a school of design directed by the sculptor Jules Lequien, who, for three years, had him draw various anatomical details from plaster casts after the antique. Some of Seurat's male nudes done between

* See p. 87.
** An early form of cartoon strip.

7

*The Gleaner. Peasant Gathering Plants, 1881–82. Black chalk, $12^{3}/_{16}'' \times 9^{5}/_{16}''$ (31.4×23.7 cm)
The British Museum, London*

FARM LABORER WITH HOE, 1882. Oil on canvas, 18¼″ × 22⅛″ (46.3 × 56.1 cm)
The Solomon R. Guggenheim Museum, New York

1875 and 1877 have been preserved; they stand out in powerful relief, whether they are copies of more famous statues such as the Antinous or simple nude studies. It was at this school that he made the acquaintance of Edmond Aman-Jean, the accomplice in art of his years of apprenticeship. In 1878 the two friends passed the examination for the Ecole des Beaux-Arts and were received in the studio of Henri Lehmann, a pupil of Ingres, « who had taken from Ingres only his most niggardly attributes, and not the vision that opens up space and forces young people to take long strides forward » (according to Aman-Jean). In spite of everything, I am convinced that Lehmann's influence on Seurat was greater than is generally thought. Sixty-four years old at the time, this society portrait painter, who had become fashionable through his portrait of the Princess Belgiojoso under Louis-Philippe, was also a fresco painter who had decorated the festival room of the City Hall (where his fifty-six panels, depicting man's work down through the centuries, were destroyed under the Commune), and two hemicycles of the Palais du Luxembourg. A perfectionist to such an extent, he had his decoration of Saint Clotilde effaced after he had executed it, judging it unworthy of him. Because of his haughty airs he was compared to a German prince (he was born in Kiel). Seurat owed to him his adoration of Ingres and his taste for technical reading matter; Lehmann read a great deal and had given himself a scientific education.

During this period the young man was drawing nudes from living models, making copies of Ingres and Ghiberti in the Louvre, using the linear treatment he had been taught by Lehmann, and was constantly delving into art books at the school library. According to his own testimony, he had already read in high school the « Grammar of Drawing » (Grammaire des Arts du Dessin) by Charles Blanc, so as to learn « the laws that should guide the painter in treating the play of colors. » He also familiarized himself with the concepts of chiaroscuro, complementary colors, achromatism, visual blending, the vibration of colors, and the color of light. He had culled from it the discoveries of Humbert de Superville on « unconditional signs of art, » and of Chevreul on « the law of simultaneous contrast. » He reconsidered these principles, and illustrated them by personal examples that were not approved by Lehmann, who ranked him forty-seventh out of eighty when he began his second year on March 18, 1979.

Seeking to perfect themselves, Seurat and Aman-Jean rented jointly a studio on the Rue de l'Arbalète, where they spent the afternoons drawing and painting still lifes and studies of men and women. It was there that Seurat made his first paintings, depicting his cousin Berthe, a woman bathing against a blue curtain, and flowers in a vase. It was there too that he executed his *Portrait of Edmond-François Aman-Jean*,* to vie with the pencil portraits of Henri Lehmann, that were held in high repute, as were those of David d'Angers and Lamennais. While his professor showed his subjects full face without any shadows, and filled the interior space between the outlines merely with a few fine lines, Seurat showed his subject in profile, painting at his easel, with his body against a solid black mass. This drawing is generally dated 1882, but Aman-Jean himself told Gustave Coquiot that it was done in the studio on the Rue de l'Arbalète. Furthermore, the pencil strokes do not resemble the rubbings in the drawings of 1882, which are studies in contrast; on the contrary, they remind one of the experimentation with chiaroscuro of the *Nude***of 1879, in which a silhouette in white stands out against a black background, the reverse of the portrait of Aman-Jean. These two drawings, larger in format than the others, were certainly created in the same year, and can verify what Charles Blanc said about « the unity of chiaroscuro » that results from the harmony between a principal light part and a dominant dark part.

In October 1879, having enlisted for one year, Seurat left for Brest to do his military service. During this time he drew in a notebook (from which there remain only fifty-six sheets), sometimes using colored pencils, barracks scenes (soldiers sleeping, mending their underwear, taking a walk), as well as studies of heads, hands and legs. In addition, he read attentively « The Phenomena of Vision, » a series of articles that David Sutter published in six issues of « Art, » beginning in January 1880, and whose aphorisms summarized « the synthesis of the science of the

---

* See p. 6.   ** See p. 82.

THE STONEBREAKER, 1882. Oil on panel, 6⅜″ × 10″ (16.2 × 25.5 cm)
The Phillips Collection, Washington, D.C.

PEASANT AT WORK, 1883. Oil on panel, 6¹¹/₁₆″ × 9⅞″ (17 × 25 cm)
Stephen Hahn Gallery, New York

The Stonebreakers, Le Raincy. c. 1881. Conté crayon, 12⅛″ × 14¾″ (30.7 × 37.5 cm)
The Museum of Modern Art, New York. Lillie P. Bliss Collection

THE STONEBREAKERS, LE RAINCY, c. 1882. Oil on canvas, 14¼″ × 17¾″ (36.2 × 45 cm)
The Norton Simon Foundation, Los Angeles

14

Peasants in the Field (Return from Labor at Sunset), c. 1883
Conté crayon, 10⁷/₈" × 12⁵/₈" (27.5 × 32 cm)
Musée du Louvre, Paris

◁
Men Walking in a Field, 1883. Conté crayon, 12" × 9¹/₈" (30.5 × 23.2 cm)
The Baltimore Museum of Art. The Cone Collection formed
by Dr. Claribel Cone and Miss Etta Cone of Baltimore, Maryland

House among Trees, 1883. Oil on wood, 6⅜″ × 9⅞″ (16 × 25 cm)
Glasgow Museums and Art Galleries

16

The Orange Vendor, 1881. Conté crayon, 12¹³/₁₆″ × 9½″ (31 × 24 cm)
Musée du Louvre, Paris

THE WATERING
CAN THE GARDEN
AT LE RAINCY, c. 1883
Oil on panel
9¾″ × 6″
(24.8 × 15.3 cm)
Collection:
Mr. and Mrs. Paul Mell
Upperville, Virginia

LANDSCAPE IN THE OUTSKIRTS OF PARIS, c. 1883. Oil on panel, 6¼″ × 10″ (16 × 25.5 cm)
Collection: Mr. and Mrs. Alexander Lewyt, New York

BARBIZON FOREST, c. 1882. Oil on panel, 6¼″ × 9⅞″ (16 × 25 cm)
Collection: Mr. and Mrs. Alexander Lewyt, New York

The Artist's Mother (Woman Sewing), 1882–83. Conté·crayon, 12¼" × 9½" (31 × 24 cm)
The Metropolitan Museum of Art, New York. Joseph Pulitzer Bequest

Woman Knitting, 1882.   Conté crayon, 12¼″ × 9¼″ (31.2 × 23.5 cm)
Fogg Art Museum, Harvard University, Cambridge, Massachusetts.   Grenville L. Winthrop Bequest

BANKS OF THE SEINE AT SURESNES, 1883
Oil on cradled panel, $6^{11}/_{16}'' \times 10^{7}/_{16}''$ (17 × 26.5 cm)
The Cleveland Museum of Art. Leonard C. Hanna, Jr. Collection

STUDY FOR « UNE BAIGNADE », 1883–84. Oil on panel, $6^{7}/_{8}'' \times 10^{3}/_{8}''$ (17.5 × 26.4 cm)
Nelson Gallery-Atkins Museum, Kansas City, Missouri. Nelson Fund

FISHERMEN, 1883. Oil on panel, $6\frac{1}{4}'' \times 9\frac{5}{8}''$ (15.7 × 24.4 cm)
Musées Nationaux. Pierre Lévy Bequest

Seated Boy with Straw Hat, 1882. Conté crayon drawing, 9½" × 14¼" (24.2 × 31.2 cm)
Yale University Art Gallery, New Haven. The Everett V. Meeks Fund

fine arts.» Seurat confessed that in Brest he reflected upon «certain ideas of Sutter on the art of ancient Greece» and that he adopted them. These ideas were rather formalistic; for example, Sutter, speaking of the Venus de Medici attributed to Cleomenes, stated: «The basic aesthetic characteristic of this statue is a curve that forms a knot.» But Sutter also showed Seurat the difference between warm colors and cold colors, with all of the consequences that entailed; he revealed to him that «light can ben broken up into three main constituent parts: vertical, horizontal, and diagonal,» and that «this supreme law governing the *components of light* is what achieves the harmony of the picture.» Sutter concluded: «Science removes all uncertainty, permits the artist to move about freely and in a very wide circle; furthermore, it is to do a double injustice to both art and science to believe that one necessarily excludes the other.» The management of «Art» published a disclaimer in a notation: «We do not share all of the opinions expressed by Mr. Sutter. ... We do not think that art, like language, can be reduced to a grammatical analysis.»

As for Seurat, he was persuaded that there did indeed exist a science of art, and that it was up to him to discover its laws in optics, in the chemistry of colors, as well as in the techniques employed in the composition of the masters. On his return to Paris, he rented a studio on the Rue de Chabrol, near the apartment of his mother on the Boulevard Magenta, where he would go regularly to take his evening meal; once more he saw a great deal of Aman-Jean, with whom he went on outings, sometimes to Pontaubert in Burgundy, sometimes to Chevry-Chessigny, of which his friend was a native, stopping to paint in the forest of Armainvilliers. He delved deeply into the theory of painting, and found everything valuable in this regard: he recopied a letter of Corot on tones, the precepts of Thomas Couture concerning fine shadings of tints, studied the method by which Puvis de Chavannes depicted light through *diffused clarity*, returned untiringly to the church of Saint-Sulpice to examine the frescoes of Delacroix in the chapel of the Holy Angels.

Convinced that Delacroix would reveal to him the secret of chromatism, he went everywhere the latter's pictures were being exhibited, analyzed them, and once he had gone back home, recorded his reflections in writing. On February 23, 1881, after viewing *The Fanatics of Tangiers*, he indicated how blue was combined with orange, yellow with violet. On May 6, in front of *The Sultan of Morocco Surrounded by his Court*, he concluded «that there is not much heavy brushwork, the exceedingly fine tones become even more so through the superimposition (of colors) which is quite visible»; * and he admired «two persons, in whose garments the balance of color comes from a combination of red and green.» On November 11, out of five Delacroix paintings shown together in the Goupil Gallery, he particularly noted *An Oriental*: «What is especially interesting is the manner in which this canvas is treated: marvelous values, the background not filled in at all, the coat thick with the ornementation embroidered in gold (...). It is a very personal application of the most rigorous scientific principles.» Fénéon, underlining the astonishing precision of this «text composed from memory, in the studio,» after contemplating these pictures at dealers' or even in «their display windows, while he stood on the sidewalk,» does justice to this extraordinary visual memory: «It was a case of reconstructing mentally not an arbitrary sampling, but colors coupled by Delacroix according to a definite plan, with a logic that Seurat understood and appreciated.»

Having learned from an article in «Figaro» in 1881 that a translation had just been made of «Modern Chromatics» by Ogden Nicholas Rood, a professor of physics at Columbia University in New York, Seurat immediately obtained a copy of the book, that was illustrated with a hundred and thirty drawings. Through it he found out about the experiments made by Maxwell with his polychrome disks, by Dove with his dichroscope, an apparatus that mixed the light coming from units of colored glass, and by Brücke with his shistoscope, that could be used to produce complementary colors. He steeped himself in the theory of Helmholtz on the sensitivity of the eye, according to which the feeling of white is produced «when the nerve clusters of the retina that correspond to red, green and violet are stimulated with approximately the same energy.» He

---

* In Homer, William Innes. «Seurat and the Science of Painting.» 1964, The MIT Press, Cambridge, Mass., p. 48.

studied Rood's circular chart, in which the complementary colors are placed opposite one another, white being in the center. He chiefly paid attention to Chapter IV, «Contrasts,» that made the assumption: «One can actually modify a color to a considerable degree without acting directly on it; it suffices to change the color that is adjacent to it.» The author articulated the law on the changes produced by contrast, explained why a combination of colors was pleasing or displeasing, described series of binary and ternary combinations: vermilion with blue is an excellent combination, whereas with violet it is bad, etc. Seurat copied Rood's «Contrast-Diagram,» so as to learn how to select his colors and employ them in the proportions calculated to produce the best effect.

THE GRAPHIC APPRENTICESHIP IN CONTRASTS

Seurat was struck by what Rood said about «the simple contrast of light and shadow, that is to say one in which the only elements are white, black, and the shades of intermediate gray.» Rood claimed that this contrast was the most difficult of all to achieve successfully, and that it could result in a drawing that would be superior to a picture: «The contrast between the light tones and the dark tones is as powerful as the contrast between warm and cold colors; in reality, the contrast between white and black is, after all, the most marked contrast that exists.» There are three very distinct kinds of contrasts: the contrast in *value*, that is to say the opposition of light and dark; the contrast in *hue*, that puts into play a color and its complement, red with green, yellow with violet, orange with blue; and the contrast in *line*, involving all differences in direction in relation to the horizontal. Before tackling the contrasts of hue and of line, Seurat therefore decided to experiment with the contrast in value, starting with white and black, and for that purpose began a series of drawings done with Conté crayons. He believed that if he could succeed in mastering value completely without using color, it would be that much easier, in his pictures, to darken or lighten the hues by using just the right proportions, based on an accurate appreciation of luminous values.

Gustave Kahn has divided Seurat's drawings into two groups: those that are «finished works in themselves, pursued for their own sake,» and those that are «preparations,» notations made with a composition to be painted in mind. He likewise categorized two sub-groups: one, the larger, consisting of the white and black drawings; the other including the drawings touched with color or executed entirely with colored pencils. He recognized that these drawings in color, almost all of them evoking the music hall, had «a gradation of dark shadowy lights that sought to dissolve into white and black as they moved further from the figures.» Finally, the drawings in the two groups and the sub-groups, according to him, were «done less for the lines than for the atmosphere.» This arbitrary distinction is far too simplistic and does not take into account the fundamental aim of Seurat, whose drawings were, above all, *experiments*. The painter placed himself before a sheet of paper like a scientist watching for a chemical reaction or verifying a law of physics.

For my part, I distinguish three different series in Seurat's drawings in Conté crayon, corresponding to three specific kinds of research. After several trial efforts, such as *The Reaper* and *The Orange Vendor*,* in which gray predominates and hachures are used to develop the theme, the first series brings into play *the lightening function of white*. Here, we have a diner whose white napkin, tied around his neck, «lights up» his dish, his bottle, his hand; there, we have a seated man «lighted up» by the newspaper spread across his knees; elsewhere, there is a nurse seen from the front, with the white expanse of her apron on her black skirt, or from the back, with her coif and her coat in contrasting tones. In the portrait of his mother, Seurat refined his technique to the point of having the light emanating from the figure (derived from the whiteness

---

* See p. 17.

of her collar against her black bodice) confront the exterior lights playing in the part in the hair and on the fingers. At other times the illumination comes from the background, which is given favored treatment over the face itself: a man reading with his back to the light may be a dark silhouette against a white and gray ground; women walking may be shadows standing out against a gray ground that outlines their forms. For Seurat, these experiments dictated his subjects and guided his observations. When he drew the *Place de la Concorde in Winter,** with a black carriage gliding over a pure white surface, or when he depicted a rag-and-bone man traveling over a snowy road, he was studying contrasts, not creating « impressions » of snow like some of his contemporaries. A woman seated in front of white linen drying on a line, a river over which the smoke from a steamboat rises, and other scenes of this sort were not created because he cared about their picturesque quality, but in order to demonstrate how light hues can inundate somber ones.

The second series of drawings tested *the coloring function of black.* Thus, a representation of plowing at twilight, allowing the viewer to catch a glimpse of two black silhouettes against a background of dusky sky crossed by a beam of light; the two plowers seem to be racing the falling night. Or a black colt between two black trees, against a ground of gray field and white sky. Seurat determined to just what extent dark tones could color, animate, and even brighten a scene, and employed light accents in a negative manner. *Young Girl in a « Chapeau Niniche »*** wears a white hat that is like snuffers darkening her face; her black silhouette, in a halo of white, surrounded by gray shadows, takes over the power to lighten that the whiteness here does not possess. Look at *Men Walking in a Field.**** the white trousers of the man who advances toward the spectator, in the middle of a gray field, are almost blinding; it does not « illuminate » the scene, but is there so that one can feel the difference between the black (color) of the jacket and the black (shadow) of the face. Signac, in his preface to a Seurat retrospective at Bernheim-Jeune in 1920, wrote accurately: « He creates the most beautiful painter's drawings one can imagine. Thanks to the exact science of values, one can say that these "white and black" drawings are more colorful and luminous than many a painting.»

Finally, the third series is the one in which Seurat studied *the calmness of tones*; in other words, the equality of the light and the dark, without one predominating over the other. For example, in his *Young Woman with a Drawing Pad****** the contrast between the black of her dress, the white of the paper on which she is drawing and of the feather on her hat, and the gray of the easel gives an impression of balance, bestowing on the person an air of deep serenity. This series is characterized by the variety of the inroads gray makes in the contrasting whites and blacks, and by the care taken in toning down the shades. Naturally, Seurat did not work on these three series consecutively. He alternated between them, coming to and going from one type of experimentation to the other, so that each of the series was able to profit from the experience acquired in the others. The one quality that all of these creations have in common is that in them he absolutely refuses to employ hard outlines. He was determined to draw without utilizing such lines, and he won the wager made with himself. There are masses of shadow and masses of brightness that, by interpenetrating, form the contours of people and objects.

Seurat, clearheaded and attentive, chose the moment and the pose when his model was at once darkened and illuminated by its surroundings. He sought a new graphic representation of the world, and he found it by making evident the radiations exchanged by bodies and their environs. His *Woman Sewing,******* whose head is a shadowy glow, is as truly seen as if one could discern her face; he did not need to define her features by delineating her eyes, her nose, her mouth. He showed that a person could light up or fade out, and that was enough to suggest joy or melancholy. Each drawing is a study of the climate appropriate to the thing it represents. White shadows in a black light, woolly thicknesses, dark transparencies, livid streaks under skies of ashes and soot, scenes at midday that seem to be taking place in the middle of the night, these are not merely copied from nature, but are evanescent forms of the universe of contrasts.

---

* See p. 31.   ** See p. 36.   *** See p. 14.   **** See p. 35.   ***** See p. 20.

There are no longer any boundaries between space and volume. One could say that objects are made to dissolve in the light or the shadows, as a lump of sugar will dissolve in water. The artist did not wish to conquer the world with the point of a pencil, using nimble strokes, but to accumulate shadows on a sheet of paper and, to gradate them in such a way that they encircle a person and even a whole spectacle. We now understand why the Surrealists admired Seurat's drawings so much: they were already «frottages.» While Max Ernst would rub with his crayon a sheet placed on the rough surface of a floor, Seurat rubbed the surface of the paper, rendered it expressive in itself, and took advantage of its roughness to achieve contrasts. One thing demonstrates his genius: Ordinarily, in drawings done with Conté crayons, the blacks are the filled spaces, the whites the empty ones; in Seurat's case, this formula is frequently reversed, and the white areas give the impression of being filled, the black of being empty.

One might believe one were watching a silent film on the desires and emotions of his life; yet his art never has recourse to the imaginary, it is not a transcription of his dreams, it does not permit any equivocations, any approximations, any allusions. Seurat drew what he saw, but he saw everything more intensely than other people; instead of stopping for details, he followed the path lined with unusual incidents, reverberations, reflections, eclipses. He explored matter, taking into account all of its immaterial aspects. His drawings appear to be mental images because he saw things with his mind as well as with his eyes. He achieved the feat of being equal to the greatest visionaries without indulging in fantastic invention, simply by pushing his powers of observation and his technique to a culmination.

Thus, at the age of twenty-three, in order to exercise his eye and his hand, exclusively concerned with learning to paint with light and with shadow, the painter executed drawings such as had never before been seen in the history of Western painting. After that, how maintain that there is no need of a method in order to create? A method is necessary, without any doubt, but on condition that an artist follows Seurat's example and personally impresses it on his mind, acts as his own professor, and, without letting himself be disturbed by the countercurrents of fashion and academism, develops the systematic prospection of a truth instinctively foreshadowed.

ABSTRACT REALISM

A few months after beginning to experiment with the contrast between black and white, Seurat ventured to deal with contrasts in color, in a group of pictures in a small format that he undertook at the same time he was doing drawings. These little works would be called «Tom Thumb box studies,» because he painted them on small strips of wood that he arranged in a portable box, known as a «Tom Thumb box,» that could be found at the time at painting supply stores. Seurat used a palette set up like Delacroix's, with the earth colors placed alongside the pure colors; and he brushed the panels freely with sweeping strokes, in the manner of the Barbizon landscape painters.

In Seurat's first paintings, it is noticeable that he stressed the contrast in line far more than he did the contrast in hue. When he subsequently confided to his entourage that he gave more attention to values than to lines in a picture, he was talking of something relevant only to the third phase in his evolution, when he was completely absorbed by chromatic contrasts, no longer having anything left to learn about linear contrasts. But at the beginning, wandering across woods and fields with his Tom Thumb box, he only stopped to reproduce scenes in which the curves, the angles, the horizontal and the vertical lines were strongly predominant; the lines that his pencil refused to trace, his brush traced in preference to all others. Here for example is his *Peasant Scene*, two women whose pitchforks cross each other at an angle, and his *Peasants Driving Stakes,*

* See p. 5.

RUE SAINT-VINCENT, MONTMARTRE IN SPRING, 1884
Oil on canvas, 9⅞″ × 6⅜″ (25 × 16 cm). The Fitzwilliam Museum, Cambridge, England

the subject of which was only an excuse for marking space with vertical lines. When he evoked landscapes of the suburbs, he had symmetrical forms jutting out from them; the cylinder of a factory chimney, the cone of a haystack, the rectangles of houses, the solid forms of all sorts offered by nature were treated for themselves and not to communicate a sensation of reality. In what he saw, on the one hand he was only interested in forms that combined to disclose clear-cut, rigid structures, and on the other hand he used his ingenuity to make these structures still more apparent by emphasizing them to the detriment of the total context. This abstract realism, that alters contours until there is a geometric idealization of his subject, is his hallmark, since none of his contemporaries were adopting this device at that particular time.

That is why, when he painted his series of *The Stonebreakers*, he refused to yield to the sentimentality of Millet; he did not make us pity the fate of the workers, for he believed that the painter was a man interested in three-dimensional forms, not a novelist or a moralist. He sought to pin down the beauty of a physical effort. His *Stonebreaker Stripped to his Waist* is pure movement — one cannot even see the head of his hammer, or the stone he is breaking; the attention is focused solely on the angle of his bending body and the movement of his arms. In another *Stonebreakers*, the two figures are indistinct, because he wished to draw our attention to their gestures rather than to their individual personalities. *Peasant at Work* is seen from the back, so that the viewer can perceive clearly the upward thrust of his hammer, lifted obliquely; *The Stonebreakers, Le Raincy* * are shown from the back, full face and in profile, as if the purpose were to make one understand the three possible aspects of their movements. The faces of his people are rarely visible; their expressions would risk making us take a subjective interest in them, whereas Seurat wished to isolate and examine deeply their objective function. For the painter, man was one object among many, and even less important than another object if the requirements of a picture demanded it. In another *Stonebreakers*, in the background, a barrow with its handles pointed toward the sky is a magnet drawing the eyes and diverts them from the men digging in the foreground; in yet another *Stonebreaker*, it is the wheelbarrow that is the center of attention.

Does this mean that Seurat chose to show impassivity in the face of reality, of a lack of humanity in painting? No, he simply considered that man was a bearer of signs, and that the painter's role was to show how these human signs composed a coherent visual communication system. When we look at a man through our window, we cannot see if he is intelligent, angry, starving, in love, jealous; we see only whether he is tall or short, young or old, blond or brunette, and we define his social position by his clothing or his movements. Conjecturing about anything beyond this would be hypothetical and often erroneous. Now, Seurat created a picture from *the truth of visual perception*, not from his hypotheses concerning what he looked at; he painted the mower facing the wheat field, the gardener, the man with a hoe, peasant women at work, without concocting literature on their emotions. Moreover, it was not because he liked to fish that he depicted anglers, but because he was filled with wonder at the diagonal and horizontal lines described as they cast their rods on the water. Consequently, one should not be surprised at the inexpressive face of his *Boy Seated in a Field* or at the stiffness of his *Horse*; ** this desensitizing of figures aims to achieve complete objectivity. Moreover, the life of objects captivated Seurat to such an extent that he treated them not as still lifes, but stressed their relations with space. Thus *The Watering Can* *** has a handle whose curve echoes the curve of a path in the background that joins the horizontal plane of a little wall.

When Seurat and Aman-Jean brought their early pictures to Degas, he told them: « Good. Now you have to lie. » Taking heed of this quip, they understood that truth in art needs to be sustained by the support of illusion. They also paid a visit to Puvis de Chavannes, in his studio on the Place Pigalle, that was their introduction to monumental painting. Seurat then decided to apply the law of contrasts to a canvas measuring 2 × 3 meters (6′ 6⅝″ × 9′ 9¹⁵⁄₁₆″), intended for the Salon of 1884. To prepare for this composition, evoking Parisians bathing in the Seine near

---

* See p. 13.   ** See back cover.   *** See p. 18.

30

Asnières, he did numerous drawings with Conté crayons: a man stretched out and seen from the back, a child putting his hands to his mouth to call, studies of heads, of legs, of piles of clothes, and so on. He also started painting «croquetons,» oil sketches of the site painted on the little panels of his Tom Thumb box that later served as a memory aid. He affixed them to the walls of his studio and consulted them while he was working on his canvas. These «croquetons» were approximate images, sometimes not even targeting the subject, as he felt his way around the central theme; they enabled him to decide what, in the landscape he had selected, should definitely be eliminated, what retained. Thus one does not necessarily find in each large composition all of the motifs of the «croquetons.»

Likewise, for *Bathing at Asnières,** Seurat made some preliminary «croquetons» representing respectively a boat near the bank, the two shores, the bridge at Courbevoie with the smoke from a factory, horses in the river, a garment left on the grass, boys bathing, the effect of a rainbow, a seated bather stripped to his waist,** a seated figure with clothes on,*** a rider on a horse in the water, etc. Subsequently he made a final study in oil, indicating the arrangement of the scene,

---

* See front cover.   ** See p. 22.   *** See p. 22.

Place de la Concorde, Winter, 1882–83. Conté crayon, 9⅛" × 12⅛" (23.2 × 30.7 cm)
The Solomon R. Guggenheim Museum, New York

STUDY FOR « LA GRANDE JATTE », 1884–85. Oil on panel, 6⅛″ × 9⅜″ (15.5 × 23.8 cm)
Private Collection

the placement of the figures, and the local topography. However, *Bathing* is a different work from the preliminary sketches: unexpected elements appear in it, such as the bather seen from the back whom Seurat painted from a model who posed for him in his studio.

This allegory of daily life was painted with flat strokes that were superimposed on one another (the Pointillist touches were added by Seurat in 1887), and appears duller than Impressionist painting because it employs ocher and earth colors. One does not notice that in it shadow, light, and local color are separated and contrasted in exactly the right proportions. *Bathing* was rejected for the Salon, along with many other submissions, which spurred the artists who had been refused into presenting their works jointly and founding for this purpose the «Groupe des Artistes Indépendants», which organized its own Salon, without jury or prize; the exhibition opened on May 15 in a shanty in the courtyard of the Tuileries. Because of its overly great dimensions, the canvas of Seurat was relegated to a wall of the refreshment stand, where few visitors came. The following month, a schism among the exhibitors gave rise to the «Société des Artistes Indépendants», of which Seurat became an active member, and where he met the artists who were soon to become his initial disciples: first Paul Signac, a painter twenty-one years old, his most fervent supporter, Albert Dubois-Pillet, a captain in the Horse Guards (who was to say: «Because of Seurat, and thanks to Seurat, I learned to adore painting. I owe everything to him!»); Charles Angrand, Hippolyte Petitjean and, a little later, Henri-Edmond Cross and Maximilien Luce.

THE BATTLE OF NEO-IMPRESSIONISM

Stimulated by the atmosphere created by this struggle for art, Seurat decided to paint more complex compositions, with a number of human figures, no longer employing ocher in his palette and basing his technique on «the purity of the spectral element.» He sought to reconstruct the «solar» spectrum through the medium or «spectrum» of pure color. The end of May 1884, on Ascension Day, he began both his large canvas and the series of his preparatory studies. The theme was the evocation of a Sunday afternoon on the island of Grande Jatte, an island in the Seine at Neuilly where Parisian families came to relax when the weather was fine. Seurat reconnoitered the terrain with his Tom Thumb box, becoming saturated with the light of the place, determining not only the precise location of this recreational spot, but also its environment. One of his first «croquetons» represented the Seine in springtime, as it could be seen from the Grande Jatte; others «sections,» at greater or lesser distances, of the bank and the undergrowth.

With his «croquetons,» Seurat started to develop a veritable stenography of light; his strokes, most often sweeping ones, have occasionally the aspect of spots indicating the tones; he did not hesitate to suggest a parasol by a round spot, fishermen by small sticks. He explored the topography foot by foot, sometimes painting a view of the background with a group, sometimes a panorama with a single man, sometimes a study in which the figures are variously in the shade or in the sun, seated or standing. Above all, he sought the contrasts in hues. While he was thus working on the *Grande Jatte*, Seurat had alongside him Charles Angrand, a Norman painter whom he respected. Angrand did the best black and white drawings of Neo-Impressionism, with the exception of Seurat. Angrand recounted that, as they left the island together, Seurat pointed out to him the trees of the Boulevard of Courbevoie: «Seurat took pleasure in making me see clearly that their green tops against the sky were circled with a pink halo.» Likewise, when they crossed Paris one evening after leaving a meeting of the Indépendants: «More than once along the route Seurat called my attention to the complementary halo of the gas lamps. ... His eyes were continually seeking out such contrasts. He liked to have someone share in his discoveries, and it pleased him to discuss them.»

Seurat chose the people for his canvas one by one, in the course of the successive sessions he spent observing, selecting all of the types in society for this composition in which one finds, in the words of Jules Christophe, «young girls, a nurse, an old Dantesque grandmother in a coif, a sprawling oarsman smoking his pipe, without distinction, his light trousers entirely devoured at the bottom by an implacable sun, a deep purple mongrel, a russet butterfly, a young mother and her little girl in a white dress with a salmon-colored belt, two Saint-Cyr cadets, still more young girls, one of whom is making a bouquet, a redheaded child in a blue dress, a couple with a maid carrying a baby, and, on the extreme right, a stiffly formal and scandalous couple, a young dandy giving his arm to a flashy companion who has on a leash a yellow, purple, ultramarine monkey.» «Croquetons» and drawings with Conté crayons treat each of them in detail: the Saint-Cyr cadet, the girl in white, the dog, the woman with a fishing line,* the woman in a pink skirt, the woman strolling with a parasol, etc. As studies for the couple with the monkey, Seurat made «croquetons» of the man alone, of the woman alone (his model was Céline, the sister of Aman-Jean),** then of the couple without the monkey; and he went to the Botanical Gardens to do drawings of monkeys.

Once he had concluded his advance work on all of the minute details of his composition, Seurat painted two preliminary canvases, so as to isolate the spatial characteristics of his imagery. *The Island of the Grande Jatte**** shows the place deserted, like a theater without actors; the lush green turf, with the shadows of the foliage, and the light playing on the water are the principal elements in the picture, in which the cold areas and the warm areas are rigorously delimited. The *Final Study for the Grande Jatte* (Metropolitan Museum, New York), done with sweeping thrusts of the brush, included all of the figures in their proper places. Seurat now possessed the desired specifics of the whole and the parts of his fresco of manners, and could undertake it knowing exactly what he needed to do to create it. This way of working had nothing in common with the method of a Renoir, who placed his easel in front of dancers and finished, in a few sessions, *The Moulin de la Galette.* Seurat finally concentrated his efforts as a painter of history in his studio, taking advantage of a pile of documents taken from life.

The definitive canvas of *La Grande Jatte* was ready to be exhibited at the Indépendants in March 1885; but it was impossible to have the exhibition, and Seurat went on to other works. In the summer, during his vacation in Grandcamp, a fishing village on the English Channel, he executed his first seascapes, and took pleasure in depicting great expanses of sky and sea. He painted nature in the raw, without the men who lived in it. *Sunset, Grandcamp* sets a strip of sky and a strip of sea against one another; *Seascape, Grandcamp* combines sky, earth and sea in a unified impression of infinite solitude. Small and large sailboats animate these seascapes, but nothing human is to be seen in them. The three small boats on the shore, in *Low Tide, Grandcamp*, seem like the carapaces of dead crustaceans, and in *Fishing Boats, High Tide*, he evoked primarily the contrast between horizontal and vertical lines. It is generally believed that lyricism is characteristic of wild and feverish individuals, who express themselves in poetry by a vehemently exclamatory style, in painting by an extravagant and unsystematic technique. Seurat is the perfect example of cold lyricism. He was enthusiastic about what he saw, but he refused to parade his enthusiasm and his passion; rather, he concealed it under the mask of geometry.

The seascapes of Grandcamp bear witness to his research in the field of harmonic triangulation. In *The Bay of Grandcamp* (Collection: Mr. and Mrs. David Rockefeller, New York), a triangle of verdure, in the center and the foreground, counterbalances the triangles of the sails; in *Grandcamp, Evening,***** a triangle of earth contrasts with the steps of a stairway forming an angle on a horizontal base. *Le Bec du Hoc,****** the most significant picture in this series, was preceded by a «croqueton» in which the horizon was barely visible, with two black triangles on the sea, to the right. In the final version, the sky was higher, the sharp point of the rock was crowned by sea gulls in flight, forming a Y, which heightened the tension and the equilibrium of the rocky mass.

The variety of the brushstrokes also characterizes the seascapes of Grandcamp: specks for the earth, vertical strokes for the rocks, horizontal dashes for the sea, etc. In *Boats, Low Tide, Grandcamp,******* as in *Le Bec du Hoc*, we can observe an innovation: Pointillism. No one has

---

* See p. 39.   ** See p. 37.   *** See p. 40.   **** See p. 50.   ***** See p. 54.   ****** See p. 55.

Young Woman with a Drawing Pad, c. 1884. Conté crayon on whitewash, 11½″ × 8½″ (29.3 × 21.7 cm)
Fogg Art Museum, Harvard University, Cambridge, Massachusetts. Collection of Maurice Wertheim

WOMAN WITH
THE MONKEY, 1884
Oil on wood panel
9¾″ × 6¼″
(24.8 × 16 cm)
mith College Museum
of Art, Northampton,
Massachusetts

ag Girl
«Chapeau Niniche»
83
é crayon
″ × 9½″
8 × 24.2 cm)
ate Collection
York

WOMEN NEAR THE WATER, 1884–85. Oil on panel, $6^{1/4}'' \times 9^{7/8}''$ (15.7 × 25 cm)
Private Collection

38

WOMAN FISHING (STUDY FOR « LA GRANDE JATTE »), c. 1884–85
Oil on panel, 6½″ × 9¾″ (16.5 × 24.8 cm). Sidney Janis Gallery, New York

THE ISLAND OF «LA GRANDE JATTE», 1884. Oil on canvas, 25½″ × 31⅞″ (64.8 × 81 cm)
Private Collection

ever been able to say exactly when, how or why Seurat used tiny dots in a picture; it seems that he never confided this to anyone. It was in his seascapes of Grandcamp that he first began to employ this technique, but which was his first attempt? And what gave him the idea? I presume that it was his drawings in black and white that logically led him to the Pointillist pictures. It is to be noted that his rubbings with his Conté crayons on paper with a rough texture gave the impression that solids were compact masses of black and white dots. Seurat wanted to transfer the texture he had achieved in his drawings to his painting, and thus to be assured of a clear, regular and accurate development of contrasts in color.

When he returned from Grandcamp to Paris, Seurat had made a new discovery in the area of pictorial science: the point. He once again took up his canvas of *La Grande Jatte* so as to go over it completely, using a method that would henceforth be fully realized, and would possess what he called «two originalities» (aesthetics and technique). During all that winter he concentrated on a painstaking stippling that changed the atmosphere and the figures of his composition. The tiny points, intended to distribute light more effectively, gave to his canvas the solemn aspect of the tomb of Rekhmire in Thebes. By applying dots of color over such a large surface, Seurat necessarily had to experience a sort of hypnotic vertigo, similar to that of the medium Joseph Crépin, who from 1939 to 1948 covered his pictures with «nailheads of color,» attaining the rate to 1500 points an hour. Simultaneously with his adorning of *La Grande Jatte* with points, Seurat experienced an evolution of auto-hypnosis that I have analyzed in «Surrealism and Dreams» (and which is compatible, as I have proved, with the spirit of scientific experimentation). Thus he transferred to his subjects the trance-like state that held him in thrall, and made of them sleepwalkers of pleasure.

Soon the news spread among his friends that he was dividing tones while employing a different touch from the comma-like touches of the Impressionists. His studio neighbor, Signac, borrowed from him this revolutionary manner of painting. Pissarro, who made the acquaintance of Seurat in October, began creating Pointillist pictures at the beginning of 1886, carrying with him along the same path his son Lucien and the latter's friend, Louis Hayet. It was agreed that Seurat, Signac and Pissarro would present their works jointly in the same room at the time of the VIIIth Exhibition of Impressionists that Degas was organizing on the first floor of the Maison Dorée, Rue Lafitte, where there was a restaurant on the ground floor. As soon as they learned which canvas Seurat intended to exhibit, Renoir, Monet, Sisley, and Caillebotte withdrew from the exhibition; they urged Pissarro to do likewise, but he refused. Degas became unwilling to put this collection under the aegis of Impressionism, and simply called it the «VIIIth Exhibition of Painting.» Assembled were drawings by Odilon Redon, landscapes by David Estoppey and Zandomeneghi, pastels by Degas, various works by Gauguin, Guillaumin, Forain, Berthe Morisot, and Mary Cassatt around the corner reserved for Seurat, Signac, and the Pissarros, father and son. Of the lot, the Parisian public noticed only a single canvas, just one, and retained only a single name: Seurat.

La Grande Jatte, * exhibited in a room so small there was really no perspective, between *Le Bec du Hoc* and *The Bay of Grandcamp*, caused an uproar. The public paraded before it without a break, to make fun of the way the composition was painted and of its «wooden figures», the couple with the monkey arousing the most hilarity. Every day the society painter, Alfred Stevens, enlisted customers of the Tortoni café and took them to the Maison Dorée to jeer at Seurat's work. Even the Naturalist writers, who had defended Manet against the world, inveighed against the newcomer. Huysmans was indignant. «Too much stylistic trickery and systemization, not enough fire emitting sparks, not enough life!» Octave Mirbeau was sad. «I have not the heart to laugh before his huge and detestable picture, which resembles an Egyptian fantasy.» Fortunately, a few visitors were enthusiastic, among others Félix Fénéon, twenty-five years old, employed at the War Ministry, editor-in-chief of the «Revue indépendante,» a phlegmatic

---

* See pp. 46–47.

nonconformist who, with a stovepipe hat on his head and a goatee, managed to look like a Yankee imitating a caricature of Uncle Sam. He was immediately enchanted by Pointillist painting, in which he saw «an inventive technical reform,» and put his caustic wit to use publicizing Seurat (who wrote him on June 24, 1890: «Among 30 articles calling me an innovator, I count 6 by you.»)

That year a group of poets in Paris had undertaken to combat the Naturalism of Zola and the Goncourts by founding the Symbolist school; even before Jean Moréas published the Symbolist Manifesto, on September 18, 1886, the magazine «La Vogue,» under the aegis of Gustave Kahn, focused on the new movement. As the Naturalists had supported the pioneers of Impressionism and disparaged Seurat, the Symbolists found it altogether natural to do just the contrary. In the June issue of «La Vogue,» Fénéon criticized the elders who clung to «Impressionism as it was already defined in previous exhibitions,» analyzed the bold innovations of La Grande Jatte and, after also praising the Pointillist landscapes, declared: «It is the highlight and most freshly interesting section of the exhibition on the Rue Lafitte, that luminous. room where, in white frames, the heavens, ablaze, spread boundlessly.» Since Seurat's praises were thus sung in «La Vogue,» which shortly afterward published «Illuminations» of Rimbaud, it is not astonishing that the painter was considered a poet.

Félix Fénéon introduced to Seurat a twenty-seven-year-old Alsatian scholar, Charles Henry, librarian at the Sorbonne; he was both erudite and an inventor, who was attempting to clarify «the mathematical laws governing sensations.» He had already invented an olfactometer that measured the perceptions of smell, and a dust catcher (the ancestor of the vacuum cleaner), a device with blades set in motion by a clockwork mechanism. Signac described «his tall blond body, clothed in greenish homespun, with a gray hat, a tie in a Liberty old rose print, and a boutonniere in his lapel»; but when Seurat met him, Charles Henry, like the artist himself, was wearing a black suit and a top hat. This extraordinary person was famous among the Symbolists because of his article of 1885, «Introduction to Scientific Aesthetics,» in which he said: «The problem of the aesthetics of forms evidently comes down to this: What are the most agreeable sort of lines? Yet a little reflection quickly establishes that the line is an abstraction; it is the synthesis of two parallel and opposite directions that enables one to trace it; the reality is the direction (. . .) The problem thus boils down to this new question: What are agreeable directions? What are disagreeable directions? In other words, what directions do we associate with pleasure and pain?»

Seurat discovered that this text advocated, in order to «prevent linear dissonances,» that one «indicate the role of direction in the geometric figures.» Through it he learned how to effect changes in direction by the science of rhythm and tempo, and how to subordinate hues to them. «There is only a single appropriate direction for a color.» Charles Henry as a scholar was similar to what Seurat was as an artist; to study one enables a person better to understand the other. They are spiritual twin brothers. As early as 1886, their names were linked in the «Little Directory of Arts and Letters,» a dictionary of contemporary celebrities compiled by the Symbolists. It stated that Charles Henry «reduces the pictures of Degas to equations,» and it gave this description of Seurat: «With his brush he paints water that flows, verdure in relief, and air that synthesizes all these elements.»

La Grande Jatte enraptured another spectator at the Maison Dorée, Emile Verhaeren, who had just published his first collection, «Les Flamandes» («The Flemings»). He said: «The unexpectedness of such art first stimulated my curiosity. Never for an instant did I doubt the complete sincerity and the exceptional innovation that were so patent and were there for me to see. I spoke about it to some artists that evening, but they scoffed at me, laughing and joking.» Verhaeren was not discouraged. «The next day I returned to the Rue Lafitte. La Grande Jatte appeared to me to be an immense step forward in the research on the purest light. No clash; an even atmosphere; passage from one plane to the other without a hitch; above all, an intangible quality to the air.» The Belgian attorney Octave Maus, the founder of «Art moderne,» also was so completely stunned that he decided to invite Seurat to exhibit in the Salon of the XX, in Brussels, of which he was the secretary.

The Nurse, 1884–85. Conté crayon, 9" × 12" (23 × 30.5 cm)
Albright-Knox Art Gallery, Buffalo, New York. Gift of A. Conger Goodyear

Since 1884, the Cercle des XX (Twenty) had organized three *avant-garde* exhibitions in the Palais des Beaux-Arts in Brussels. Madeleine Octave Maus wrote: «The 1887 show is presented solely under the insignia of *La Grande Jatte*; I do not say, "of Seurat," but of this work alone; so many riots did it incite, so many battles did it bring about, that it diverted the attention of the public from the six landscapes of Honfleur and Grandcamp.» From then on Seurat's career progressed simultaneously in France and in Belgium, for in both countries his admirers followed his evolution with excitement.

Seurat found himself elevated to the position of head of a school in spite of himself, having neither the ambition nor the temperament. Not at all belligerent and group-minded like Signac, on the contrary he was taciturn, distant, introspective, never pushing himself forward at a gathering. At meetings of the Société des Indépendants at the Café Marengo, near the Louvre, he invariably seated himself in the same place against the wall and smoked his tiny pipe while listening to his comrades. Verhaeren found him «shy and silent» and said: «We had to break a great many cakes of ice before we could reach out to one another.» When he succeeded in taming the artist, in the course of a visit to his studio, Seurat spoke to him for the most part, in a monotonous voice and in didactic terms, of «his base,» that is to say of all of the results obtained by testing his principles. This ascetic of art, of an imperturbable seriousness, was preoccupied only with perfecting himself.

Furthermore, Seurat was even less inclined to be the leader of Neo-Impressionism because he considered his method to be a personal invention, conceived for him alone to use. He reluctantly allowed others to adopt it, on the express condition that they recognize that he had priority. He was angry about a biography of Pissarro that stated that «a friend of Mr. Henry, the painter Georges Seurat,» had taught him «the mathematical rules governing the division of tones.» That presupposed that Seurat had not known these rules before meeting Henry. «If I was unknown before '85, I existed nonetheless, I and my vision,» he protested. His extreme sensitivity made him resentful of the proselytism of Signac, who gave receptions every Monday so that he could pontificate on the new style. «The more there are of us, the less original we will be,» Seurat warned. Yet this attitude was not inspired by any arrogant feeling as to his own worth, since Seurat wrote to Verhaeren, when asking for the return of the canvases he had exhibited at the Salon des XX: «Ask Mr. Maus to take good care of my packages and the *rolling up* of my bombastic painting.» What Seurat irreverently called his «bombastic painting» was nothing less than that masterpiece, *La Grande Jatte*; perhaps he was proud of his method, but he remained modest about his execution of it and believed he had constantly to try to do better.

CHROMO-LUMINARISM

There was need of a name for this pictorial revolution. The men about town called it Confetti-ism, certain critics labelled it Pointillism, and an article in «Figaro,» of July 4, 1886, baptized Seurat and his disciples «Tachists.» Such descriptions made the mistake of persuading people that the principal element in the technique was the point and not the division of tones; that is why Seurat would later adopt the term, Divisionism, and treat the Pointillists like common imitators who did not divide their canvases according to the law of simultaneous contrast. On September 19, 1886, in «Art moderne,» Félix Fénéon gained acceptance for the word, «Neo-Impressionism,» which had still another weakness, in that it presented the new movement as an offshoot of Impressionism, the result simply of a quarrel between the «romantic Impressionists» and the «scientific Impressionists.» Seurat, not happy with any of these successive appelations, chose, in July, 1887, to call himself a «Luminarist.» Subsequently his style was referred to as Chromo-Luminarism, a name that he may not have been the first to use (it seems that Alphonse Germain can lay claim to that) but to which the Neo-Impressionists themselves asserted their rights in 1891, in order to distinguish themselves from the Neo-Traditionalists who, rejecting science, wanted to paint in the manner of the Primitives.

Chromo-Luminarism is the art of practising painting with «colored lights,» utilizing «pigmentary colors» in their pure state. The picture will then appear to be done, not with coloring matter, but with beams of colored light. This impression is obtained through the contrasts of value and hue, value being defined as «a high degree of luminous intensity, or a modification such as a color might undergo in order to produce light and dark,» and hue as «each spectral color and its complement, or more learnedly: the degree of refrangibility, the wave length of a colored light.» A colored light is distinguished by its value, its hue, and its «luminosity» (a quality peculiar to each value and that varies accordingly). In addition a pigmentary color should possess «purity,» such purity being the absence of any alteration in its chromatic characteristics. Seurat did not mix his pigmentary colors with one another, and did not superimpose them even according to the law of successive contrast, since he wished to avoid «muddying» his colors.

He juxtaposed on the canvas only colors in the solar spectrum, adding to them the amount of white necessary to gradate the tints. He wrote, in a working memo: «Putting white alongside a color is to bring out its value, it is to act as if one were removing from the color the white light that weakens its intensity.» His method called for an enormous virtuosity in the application of

STUDY FOR SUNDAY AFTERNOON ON THE ISLAND OF « LA GRANDE JATTE », 1884–85
Oil on canvas, 6⅛″ × 9½″ (15.6 × 24.1 cm)
The Metropolitan Museum of Art, New York. Robert Lehman Collection

SUNDAY AFTERNOON ON THE ISLAND OF « LA GRANDE JATTE », 1884–86
Oil on canvas, 81″ × 120⅜″ (205.7 × 305.8 cm)
The Art Institute of Chicago. Collection Helen Birch Bartlett Memorial

THE SEINE AT « LA GRANDE JATTE » IN THE SPRING, 1887
Oil on canvas, 25⅝″ × 31⅞″ (65 × 82 cm)
Musées Royaux des Beaux-Arts de Belgique, Art Moderne, Brussels

« La Grenouillère », c. 1885. Conté crayon, 9³/₈" × 12¹/₈" (23.8 × 30.8 cm)
Museum of Art, Rhode Island School of Design. Gift of Mrs. Murray S. Danforth

THE CHANNEL AT GRANDCAMP, 1885. Oil on canvas, 25½″ × 32″ (64.8 × 81.3 cm)
Private Collection

END OF THE JETTY AT HONFLEUR, 1886. Oil on canvas, 31⅞″ × 25⅝″ (81 × 65 cm)
Rijksmuseum Kröller-Müller, Otterlo, Netherland

values; that is why his palette contained a wide assortment of pure colors (hues), an assortment of colors mixed with white (values), and an assortment of whites.

Although one critic of the period described Seurat as «the veritable apostle of the lentil,» it is not the touch in the form of a lentil that characterizes Chromo-Luminarism; it is the separation of the colored elements. The innovation made by Seurat was the unfailing linkage of the divison of values to the law of complements; but Mile had demonstrated in 1839 that the division of values could be achieved by means of fine parallel lines. Seurat's Pointillism does not represent progress except if one takes into account the whole of his system. The picture was composed of little circular spots corresponding: 1) to the local color of the object seen close by; 2) to the light of the sun reflected without alteration on its surface, that is generally on orange shade; 3) to the light of the sun partially absorbed by the surface and whose hue is thereby modified; 4) to the reflections projected or the object by neighboring objects; 5) to the complements of the surrounding colors. Thus Chromo-Luminarism analyzes very precisely the effect of light in space. The synthesis occurs on the retina of the spectator, through an optical blend, some distance away. «Take two steps backward, and all of those multicolored drops dissolve into flowing luminous masses,» declared Fénéon.

If Seurat had confined his efforts to making his colors as brilliant as possible, he would no longer cause us to marvel, for today we do not see his pictures as he painted them. With the pigments delivered by his supplier, Edouard, he was not always able to obtain the purity he desired. As early as 1892, Fénéon recognized, viewing *La Grande Jatte*, that, even though the blues and pinks had remained unchanged, «the orange shades that are supposed to represent light represent only holes.» And yet Seurat's painting still retains its mysterious seductiveness because it is based primarily on the axiom: «Art in Harmony.» Now Harmony is born from the reconciliation of opposites, the similarities between luminous and spatial values, the equilibrium between the physical and the moral; consequently, Harmony in painting depends on the simultaneous contrasts between hues, values, and lines, and also from its subordination to one of the three emotions that govern the feelings of man about nature and about himself: gaiety, serenity and sadness. According to Seurat, a painter should know how to harmonize a gay value, a gay hue and a gay line; a serene value, a serene hue and a serene line; a sad value, a sad hue and a sad line. He will combine gaiety with sadness or serenity (of value, of hue or of line) only as a function of the science of contrasts, to set off the predominant characteristic of the picture better.

The «Chromo-Luminarist Theory,» published in the periodical, «La Plume» (No. 57, September 1891), stated that Seurat had invented «a syntax of pictorial harmonization,» in accordance with the following synoptic schema:

VALUES		HUES		LINES	
Harmony of serenity, produced by light and dark in equal proportions		Warm and cold in equal proportions		Horizontal	
Harmony of gaiety . . . . luminosity predominant	and their complementary values	warm predominant	and their complementary hues	rising	and their complementary directions
Harmony of sadness . . . . dark predominant		cold predominant		falling	

Charles Henry contributed to Seurat's Luminarism by constructing a chromatic circle that apportioned colors according to their decreasing wave lengths, when one turned beginning at the top where red was located, toward the right where orange, yellow and green succeeded one another; below was the blue-green, followed to the left as one went back up by pure blue, violet-blue and violet. The value of each hue went from light to dark from the center to the periphery; the saturated color was in the center of the area. The chromatic circle enabled the artist to compare the continuous cycle of colors that evoked a luminous sensation with the discontinuous cycle of

SHORE AT BAS-BUTIN, HONFLEUR, 1886. Oil on canvas, 26³/₈″ × 30³/₄″ (67 × 78 cm)
Musée des Beaux-Arts, Tournai. Vancutsem Collection

THE « BEC DU HOC », GRANDCAMP, 1885. Oil on canvas, 25½″ × 32⅛″ (64.8 × 81.7 cm)
The Tate Gallery, London

Boats, Low Tide, Grandcamp, 1885. Oil on canvas, 32½″ × 25¾″ (82.6 × 65.5 cm)
Private Collection

La Maria at Honfleur, 1886. Oil on canvas, $21^{7}/_{16}"\times25^{3}/_{8}"$ (54.5 × 64.5 cm)
Prague Museum

Study for «The Models», c. 1887. Charcoal, 11^{11}/$_{16}$" × 8^{13}/$_{16}$" (29.7 × 22.5 cm)
The Metropolitan Museum of Art, New York. Robert Lehman Collection

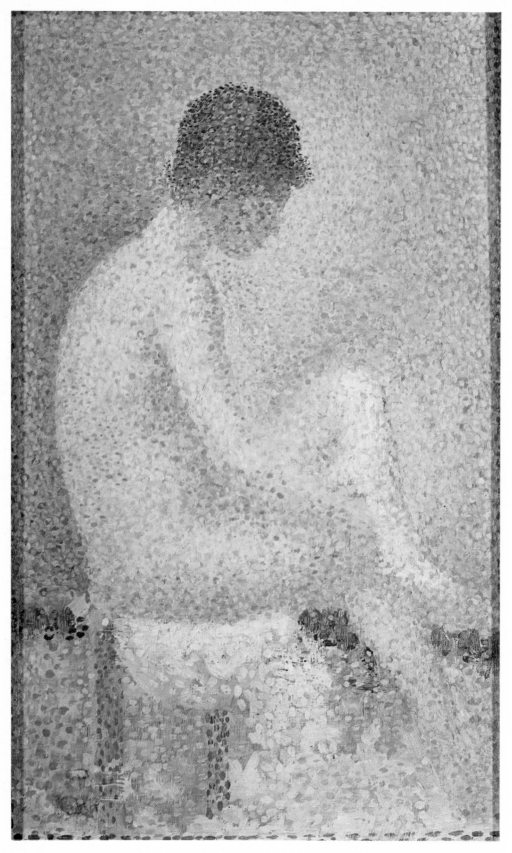

SEATED MODEL
(STUDY FOR
« THE MODELS »)
1886–87
Oil on panel
$9^{1}/_{2}'' \times 5^{7}/_{8}''$ (24 × 15
Musée du Louvre
Jeu de Paume, Paris

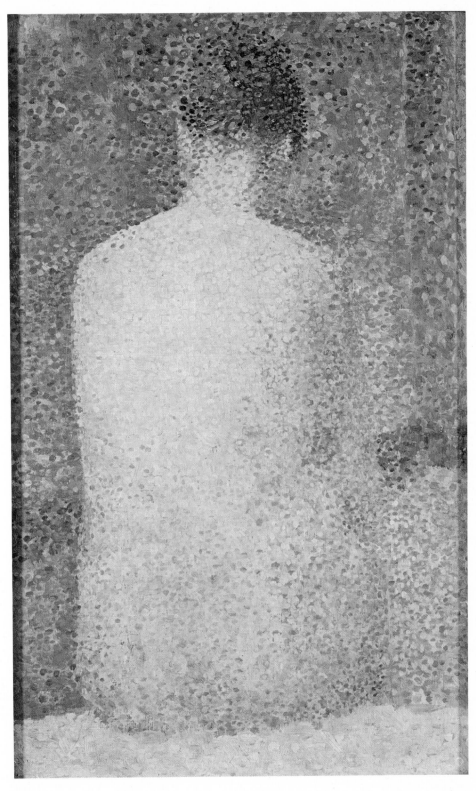

Seated Model, Back (Study for « The Models »), 1887
Oil on panel, 9⅝″ × 6¼″ (24.5 × 15.5 cm)
Musée du Louvre, Jeu de Paume, Paris

Theatre Stage, 1887–88. *Conté crayon,* 12³/₁₆″ × 8½″ *(31 × 21.5 cm)*
Musée du Louvre, Paris

Café Singer, 1887–88. Drawing on Gillot paper, with gouache highlights, 11¾″ × 9″ (29.7 × 22.9 cm)
Rijksmuseum Vincent van Gogh, Amsterdam

Café-Concert, 1887. Conté crayon with white heightening on Ingres paper, 12″ × 9¼″ (30.5 × 23.5 cm)
Museum of Art, Rhode Island School of Design. Gift of Mrs. Murray S. Danforth

At the «Concert Européen», 1887–88. Conté crayon, 12¼″ × 9⅜″ (31.1 × 23.8 cm)
The Museum of Modern Art, New York. Lillie P. Bliss Collection

colors that related to form. He could perceive how to combine them correctly with their complements, that vary depending on whether it is a question of the three primary lights or the four basic pigments.

After having initiated Chromo-Luminarism in *La Grande Jatte*, Seurat established a rhythm in his work pattern that he explained to Verhaeren. His pattern consisted of doing a «large, experimental and, if possible, innovative canvas each winter.» In the summer, he would work at the seashore, to «wash out of his eyes the shadows of days spent in the studio,» to observe nature and study light. This program brought him to Honfleur in June, 1886, where he painted a series of seascapes in a more sharply defined style than those of Grandcamp. The brushstrokes enclosed the landscape in a tight network of points, the atmosphere seems made of a dusting of soft light. In them he subtly recreated the variations in climate, the effect of a sunset, in *Evening, at Honfleur*, and an overcast sky in *End of the Jetty at Honfleur,** in which the rigidity of the lighthouse to the left contrasts with the nebulousness of the grayish air.

The Honfleur seascapes are serenely harmonious, expressing life without drama, reality not animated by humans, the immutable and the eternal. Man is present in them only through his works: the lighthouse, the quay, the house, the boat. It makes the viewer aware of the dialogue between the earth and the sea, one representing a refuge, the other adventure. Thus, *The Shore at Bas-Butin, Honfleur*** offers a simple confrontation between a rising coastal mass and a vista toward the open sea: fullness and emptiness face to face. Seurat paid homage to the stability of things; that is why, in *Entrance to the Harbor, Honfleur*, the whole focus of the picture is on a mooring cleat in the foreground, whose solidity contrasts with the dependency of a sail hollowed into the shape of a crescent moon, in the background. That is also why he portrayed so lovingly the rigging of boats at anchor, stable combinations of verticals, horizontals and curves, as in *La Maria, Honfleur,**** an anatomical study of a ship alongside the quay. The precision of his work was such that a sketch painted in a week, *Corner of a Dock*, appears to us as much a completed work as *The Lighthouse at Honfleur*, that the executed in two and a half months, paying the most careful attention to the density of forms.

Seurat's Honfleur seascapes pleased the Naturalists, even Huysmans, who praised the painter for «the feeling he expresses of a nature that is drowsy rather than melancholy, of a nature that rests peacefully under a firmament devoid of rage, sheltered from the wind.» Strengthened by this new experiment, Seurat henceforth treated the landscape with handsome Pointillist arrangements, as in *The Seine at Courbevoie* and *The Bridge at Courbevoie,***** adding as a vibrant note a girl walking or anglers who become part of the momentum of the verticals and horizontals of the urban site represented.

The detractors of Neo-Impressionism claimed that Seurat's method, even though it enabled him to do successful seascapes, could not be applied equally successfully to the human figure. In order to demonstrate to them that they were wrong, he decided that his entry in the lists in the winter of 1886 would be a nude, but not just any sort of nude: a classical nude, in the style of Ingres' bathers, whose only modernity would be derived from the division of tones and the Pointillist brushstrokes. As the successful execution of a single nude might be attributed to a fortunate happenstance, he resolved to include three in the same composition, using different poses that hinted at as many technical difficulties to be resolved. For *The Models* (Barnes Foundation, Merion, Pennsylvania), Seurat adopted an almost academic grouping, recalling *The Oceanids* of Henri Lehmann, who grouped four nude women around a rock, posing one full face, one in profile, one from the back, and one in a three-quarters attitude. He did not attempt a free combination of poses, to suggest the carelessness of intimacy, as an Impressionist would have done. His three models are frozen in predetermined locations, for they are there solely to show a female body seen from the back, full face and in profile, and offered the painter the opportunity to treat flesh from different points of view.

---

* See p. 51.   ** See p. 53.   *** See p. 56.   **** See p. 69.

Clowns and Pony (Sidewalk Show), c. 1882.   Conté crayon, 12½″ × 9½″ (31.8 × 24.2 cm)
The Phillips Collection, Washington, D.C.

INVITATION TO THE
SIDE-SHOW, 1887–88
Oil on canvas
39¼″ × 59″
(99.2 × 149.9 cm)
The Metropolitan Museum
of Art, New York.
Bequest of Stephen C. Clark

The Steamboat, 1886.   Charcoal on paper, 9³⁄₈″ × 12¹⁄₈″ (23.8 × 30.8 cm)
Albright-Knox Art Gallery, Buffalo, New York. Gift of A. Conger Goodyear

Seurat began by painting the figures in separate pictures, so as to study in depth each of the aspects that wold subsequently be brought together. As was his custom, he sketched a standing nude with Conté crayons to determine the luminous values, then did a «croqueton» to establish the contrast of hues, before executing his *Standing Model* (Louvre Museum, Paris), her hands crossed over her belly, a scrap of red ribbon in her hair, the whole in a nimbus of spangles of light. Jules Christophe was enthousiastic. «Absolutely irreproachable drawing, exquisite tranquillity, a rare ingenuousness and honesty; much stronger than the artful *Spring* of old man Ingres.» But Huysmans, who in March 1887 saw the *Standing Model* at the Indépendants, grumbled: «Peel away from his models the colored fleas that cover them, and underneath there is nothing: no

THE BRIDGE AT COURBEVOIE, 1886–87. Oil on canvas, 18″ × 21½″ (46 × 55 cm)
Courtauld Institute Galleries, London

PORT-EN-BESSIN, 1888
Oil on canvas
$26^3/_8'' \times 33^3/_{16}''$
$(67 \times 84.3$ cm)
The Minneapolis Institute
of Arts.
The William Hood
Dunwoody Fund

PORT-EN-BESSIN: THE OUTER HARBOR (LOW TIDE), 1888
Oil on canvas, 20¾″ × 25⅞″ (53.7 × 65.7 cm)
The Saint Louis Art Museum, Missouri

PORT-EN-BESSIN, ENTRANCE TO THE HARBOR, 1888
Oil on canvas, 21⅝″ × 25⅝″ (55 × 65 cm)
The Museum of Modern Art, New York. Lillie P. Bliss Collection

Seascape at Port-en-Bessin, Normandy, 1888. Oil on canvas, 25½″ × 31¾″ (64.8 × 80.7 cm)
National Gallery of Art, Washington, D.C.
Gift of the W. Averell Harriman Foundation in memory of Marie N. Harriman

74

Port-en-Bessin: The Outer Harbor (High Tide), 1888
Oil on canvas, 26³⁄₈″ × 32¹⁄₄″ (67 × 82 cm)
Musée du Louvre, Jeu de Paume, Paris

Sᴜɴᴅᴀʏ ᴀᴛ Pᴏʀᴛ-ᴇɴ-Bᴇꜱꜱɪɴ, 1888. Oil on canvas, 25⅝″ × 31⅞″ (65 × 81 cm)
Rijksmuseum Kröller-Müller, Otterlo, Netherlands

soul, no thought, nothing. An emptiness in a body of which only the contours exist.» The *Seated Model, Profile*,* with her body blending so admirably into the surrounding atmosphere, and the *Seated Model, Back*** were not calculated to mollify the writer, who demanded that a picture express the verity of life, whereas Seurat wanted from then on to establish the verity of colored space.

The Models should really have been called *The Model*, for it is the same model who is seen in the three poses, as in a «simultaneist» work. The gaze is confined to a space between two sections of walls, and invited to contemplate spectral nudities; the woman in the center is the bisector of a triangle whose two sides are occupied by the woman seen from the back and the one who is putting on her stockings. On the ground and on stools, hats with feathers, a fan, boots, corsets, an orange, flowers multiply the contrasts. Fénéon noted: «Through a pseudo-scientific fantasy, the red parasol, the yellow parasol and the green stocking are oriented in the direction where the red, the yellow and the green are located in Henry's chromatic circle.» This superb piece caused contradictory reactions among the Impressionists. «Ah, my dear brother, if only I could do something like that!» Van Gogh wrote to Théo, recalling that he had seen, before departing for Arles, *The Models* at Seurat's. He added: «The leader of the "Petit Boulevard" is undoubtedly Seurat.» (Van Gogh called the group of innovators of which he was a member the «Petit Boulevard»; for him, the «Grand Boulevard» was Renoir and his friends.) But Renoir, discovering *The Models* at Vollard's in 1887, exploded in indignation, as Signac reported. «Renoir, it appears, was horrified by the picture; he found it idiotic, ridiculous, and saw in it nothing, nothing, nothing at all.»

Seurat worked slowly on *The Models*, complaining about the changes in his colors because of the bad pigments. In August 1887, he wrote Signac from Paris: «Plastered canvas extremely discouraging. No longer understand anything. Everything spots and smudges — work painful.» Before he had yet completed *The Models*, during the winter of 1887 he started *Invitation to the Side-Show*, and thus undertook at the same time two works that were diametrically opposed, the first warm, the second cold. Seurat regularly attended the street shows given at the fair in Neuilly and the Foire du Trône, that took place at night. He made sketches of jugglers in the booths where Señorita Rosita de la Plata, jockey, and Miss Adrienne Anciou, the queen of the air, appeared; but he eliminated the anecdotal and painted only the prelude to this sort of attraction.

*Invitation to the Side-Show*** has a sad harmony; because the solid parts are arranged with rigorous symmetry. In the interior of the imperfect rectangle of the frame, Seurat traced a «rectangle of gold,» bounded at the top by the line where nine gas lamps cause their flowers of fire to bloom. The trombone player in the center, wearing a conical hat, divides this perfect rectangle into two sections of equal importance. The orientation of the picture from left to right is assured by the lower branch of the tree, that clearly points up the right, and by the head of the clown turned in that direction. On the other hand, the stage manager, a cane under his arm and thrusting out his chest, arrests this movement toward the right (note the subtle curve of his belly that sets off the movement just expressed and halts it) and, through his profile and his general attitude, persuades us to go back toward the left. Thus the composition was once more put into balance, uniting the static and the dynamic. The three clarinet players spread melancholy through the descending lines of their instruments. In the foreground, a procession of men's and women's heads curves inward as it passes, framing the scene nicely. Five luminous reflections, shining in the glass panes above the stage manager, draw our attention to him, whereas otherwise it might be focused on the five clowns on the platform.

This picture is a marvel of equilibrium, for nothing in it is favored over anything else, neither the left nor the right, neither the top nor the bottom, neither the foreground nor the background; everything is stressed with the same intensity. A monotone gamut ranging from cold blues to violets expresses the sadness of the night. The gaiety of the spectacle to which the sightseers have been invited is suggested by the reddish, violet and yellow background behind the

---

* See p. 58.   ** See p. 59.   *** See pp. 66–67.

trombone player, and the orange, blue, green and yellow nimbus around the clarinetists, yet the blue frill of the clown and the greens of the jambs of the door near the stage manager dampen this impression of human warmth. The image is constructed in such a way as to be ambiguous, to contain a mixture of anguish and of pleasure; hope in some to have fun; fear to disappoint or be disappointed; the vague feeling that the night carries the threat of solitude that must be exorcised by throwing oneself into the whirling of a spectacle.

«THE ART OF HOLLOWING OUT A SURFACE»

The Pointillist brushstroke appeared to Pissarro to be the greatest difficulty of Chromo-Luminarism, as he indicated in a letter of September 6, 1888, to his son. «What can one do to obtain the qualities of purity, simplicity in the dots, and the body, the suppleness, the freedom, the spontaneity, the freshness of sensation of our Impressionist art? That is the question; it preoccupies me a great deal, for the point is thin, without consistency, transparent, monotonous rather than simple even in Seurat's case, especially in Seurat's case.» For his part, Seurat must have asked himself the same question, if one can judge by his summer landscapes of 1888 done at Port-en-Bessin, in which he sought above all the mellowness of matter, and did not let points be the dominant feature. One of them, *Port-en-Bessin: The Outer Harbor (High Tide),* * was even painted with sweeping brushstrokes, that remained visible beneath the spaced points with which he covered them; emphasis was placed, not on the fragmented touches, but on the stylization of the thing seen. In it he was primarily interested in the alternation of filled and empty areas, through the contrast of the two parallel horizontals of the jetties, the masses of the coast, the houses and the sailboats.

Considered as a whole, the seascapes of Port-en-Bessin bear witness to his efforts to delineate firmly the geometry of nature. Some of them are constructed with a perpendicular central axis and a section of gold. Without betraying the landscape he was depicting, Seurat redistributed its various elements to make it more decorative. In *Seascape at Port-en-Bessin, Normandy* ** the clouds undulate in an ornamental pattern that echoes the undulation of the top of the coastal hill, and the solid mass of earth rising to the left acts as a foil for the sea to the right. The spatial organization of these seascapes is almost always far-reaching; the end of the horizon is indicated by a ship's masts in the distance in *Port-en-Bessin: The Outer Harbor (Low Tide),* *** but one finds a panoramic view without limits in *Port-en-Bessin, Entrance to the Harbor,* **** with its scattered sailboats, its zones of light, its complete opening-up of space. Finally, Seurat crossed the threshold of dreams in *Port-en-Bessin,* ***** a fairly disturbing landscape that enables one to understand why this painter has been associated with the Surrealists; in my opinion, it is Seurat's only Surrealistic picture, but it is so forcefully so that it heralds Chirico's *Plazas of Italy.* Its enigmatic characters — especially the petrified child, anxious about who knows what danger — the fateful bridge leading to seemingly haunted buildings, the atmosphere of mingled anticipation and lethargy, belong to a reality midway between wakefulness and sleep.

The year 1889 was a crucial one for Seurat, because painters in France and Belgium loudly proclaimed his influence. Belgian Neo-Impressionism was born in February, at the Salon of the XX in Brussels where he was the guest of honor; it was there that Théo van Rysselberghe exhibited some Chromo-Luminarist landscapes and his Pointillist portrait of Madame Edmond Picard. Seurat himself enumerated his Belgian disciples in his list of «Twenty-ists in favor of optical painting»; they were Anna Boch, Frantz Charlet, Dario de Regoyos, Jan Toorop, Henry van de Velde, Théo van Rysselberghe, Guillaume Vogels, and Georges Lemmen. This group took advantage of the advice of Gustave Kahn, who settled in Schaerbeek in Belgium and who saw to it that Neo-Impressionism merged with Symbolism.

---

* See p. 75.   ** See p. 74.   *** See p. 72.   **** See p. 73.   ***** See pp. 70–71.

It was probably in the spring of 1889 that Seurat entered into a liaison with Madeleine Knoblock, a girl of twenty, a friend of Emilie Etiembre who had served as a model for Degas' jockeys. He painted his companion in *Young Woman Powdering Herself*,* the only instance when he applied the technique of Chromo-Luminarism to a portrait. He showed a baby-faced woman-child, with radiant flesh (as a matter of fact, she was already pregnant by him), whose wide-spaced eyes, pouting expression and low brow denoted a stubborn and capricious nature. Pissarro, commenting on the gossip that she spread after the death of the painter, said: «The mistress of poor Seurat is a woman who may not be evil, but is certainly brainless.» That might explain the fact that the motifs of the mural tapestry appear to be contradictory — they have the form of arrowheads pointed downward (a sign of sadness), yet are of a clear yellow (the color of joy). Seurat suggested the intimacy of their relationship by originally tracing his own face in the mirror on the wall; however a friend, who was ignorant of their close ties, objected saying that a self-portrait placed in this painting would provoke smiles. Seurat then substituted the reflection of a flowerpot. An X-ray made in the laboratory of the Art Institute of Chicago in 1957 has enabled us to perceive underneath the sketch of the artist's head.

In June 1889 Seurat spent a brief vacation at Crotoy, where he painted two seascapes — a view of Crotoy from below, in the morning, and a view from above,** in the afternoon — having *simultaneous borders*, conceived and executed at the same time as the pictures. This marked the definitive termination of Seurat's evolution as it applied to the question of framing. First he had put his paintings in white frames, like the Impressionists, then he had noted the reactions of adjacent colors on one another by streaking the white. For a time he imagined that the frame was truly a part of the reality of the landscape and that it should be punctuated with orange or blue depending on whether the sun was behind or in front of the spectator, and the frame, supposedly, in the light or in shadow. In the two views of Crotoy, Seurat decided to paint the border on the canvas itself, utilizing only the colors that complemented the adjoining ones.

By the autumn of 1889 Seurat had created *Le Chahut (The Hullabaloo)*,*** about which André Salmon would say: «Let us remember that the first Cubist studios were decorated with photographs of Ingres and Seurat, notably of his *Chahut*, one of the principal icons of the new cult.» The scene is set in the Concert de l'Ancien Monde, a dingy cabaret on the Boulevard de Clichy where Seurat went to draw between eight o'clock and midnight; it reeked of a stench of the stable and one was bitten by fleas there, according to Gustave Coquiot, who frequented the place. «The semblance of an orchestra, the semblance of a headliner fitted in well with a semblance of men and women singers.» Before the number that ended the spectacle, male and female dancers with such first names as Gunner, Blondie, Ladybird and Hussar danced the eccentric dance, the «chahut,» that the painter has evoked so powerfully. Yet he has given us not a literal reality as he observed it, but rather a recreation of the spirit. Indeed, Coquiot has told us that the hall was very dark, having a single luminous globe, and yet Seurat has put three of them in his picture. The painter, who also executed drawings at the Eden Concert Hall and the Gaieté-Rochechouart, synthesized all his impressions of the world of café concerts to create an image of pleasure-loving Paris.

There will never be an occasion to comprehend more fully that there are two levels in Seurat's creative process: the conscious and the unconscious. The conscious is interested solely in the mathematical distribution of forms and colors, but the unconscious slyly introduces serendipitous findings permeated by his haunting concern with life's mystery. On the conscious level, Seurat wanted to surpass the poster artist Jules Chéret, whose posters for the Folies-Bergères expressed, in Huysmans's words, a «mad, almost explosive joy.» On the unconscious level, all that the austere young man experienced in these orgiastic surroundings was embodied in the devilish heat emanating from the protagonists, who seemed possessed by an infernal joyousness.

---

* See p. 83.   ** See p. 81.   *** See p. 87.

What should be noted in *Le Chahut* are the solidity of the architectonics and the logical distribution of the masses. The principal figures are assembled on the right so as to be more pleasing to the spectator, for Charles Henry had affirmed: «Going in a direction from left to right . . . is usually agreeable; it is undoubtedly for this reason that we place on our right those beings whom we wish to see and to honor.» Furthermore, the direction from bottom to top, corresponding to the viewer's pleasure, is persistently indicated by the legs of the dancers and the butterfly ribbons on the shoes of the women; it is even underlined, below, by the neck of the musician's contrabass. The cane and the hat of the spectator have a reverse orientation, so as to impart the idea of movement through the contrast in directions. «Any motion stopped while going in one direction automatically evokes the opposite direction. This direction might be called *complementary*,» said Charles Henry.

The yellow lamp on the left expresses joy rising. This decorative motif reminds us of the mural paper of *Young Woman Powdering Herself*, in which it served a negative function. One can observe the forked tail on the costume of one of the dancers, that gives him the appearance of a devil; it is the converse of an oriflamme in *Sunday, at Port-en-Bessin.* * The oriflamme was pointed down, to add a touch of melancholy to the landscape; the tail of the costume is pointed upward, to denote joy. It is apparent with what a restrained vocabulary, with how much discipline and sobriety in the use of his resources, Seurat achieved his effects; he is the most classical of the *avant-garde* painters.

It is probable that Seurat, together with Signac, attended the lecture entitled «Harmony of Forms and Colors» that Charles Henry gave on March 27, 1890 at the Forney Library. The lecturer paid tribute to Signac, who had just executed a poster using his aesthetic protractor, and specified that he did not pretend to be able to lay down infallible rules for painters. «The rational realization of beauty presupposes a fully developed science, which we are far from achieving.» What he would like to do would be «to build, on a rigorous mathematical base, a vast science: *morphology*,» and demonstrate why visual sensations can be either agreeable or disagreeable. «It is a question of constructing forms that do not fatigue the eyes, or that, on an even surface, produce the greatest possible visual sharpness.»

The seascapes that Seurat would do that summer at Gravelines in the North of France, near Calais, could be defined precisely as meditations on morphology. His channel views, stripped of nonessentials, preceded by «croquetons» and studies of details in Conté crayons, and framed by somber borders, would combine forms and directions in a manner that could achieve a serene-sad or a serene-gay expression. One could say that he made nature pose, as he made the models for his nudes pose. In *The Channel in the Gravelines Harbor, One Evening,* ** it may have been he who asked a fisherman to place on the right his two tilted anchors, to balance the vertical line of a street lamp, the horizon line, the bend of the shoreline. In *Harbor at Gravelines,* *** the two small boats to the right, whose masts slant toward the left, express repose through the contrast between an agreeable form and a disagreeable direction (in back). In *Petit Fort-Philippe,* **** the sensation of depth is achieved thanks to the listing boat that draws attention, by its slanting mast, to the recession of the quay to the right; this incline is all the more striking because everywhere else strong perpendiculars (lighthouse, central pillar, masts of the other boats) rise up from invisible horizontals.

The great climactic picture that absorbed Seurat during the winter of 1890 was *The Circus.* ***** This subject had fascinated him for a long time; already in 1880, in a notebook of sketches begun in Brest, he had drawn with colored pencils an entrance to the Corvi circus, a female dancer and a red clown. Subsequently he spent many evenings at the Fernande circus, near his home, noting all of the details of the spectacle. He would prepare for *The Circus* by drawings with Conté crayons (one of them, the profile of a clown, stands out against a geometric tracing), and even by a watercolor featuring the ringmaster. In the complete study in oil, the dots are widely separated, the silhouettes roughed out; the right hand of the clown, seen from the back, makes a different

---

* See p. 76.   ** See p. 91.   *** See p. 89.   **** See p. 90.   ***** See p. 86.

VIEW OF « LE CROTOY », FROM UPSTREAM, 1889
Oil on canvas, 27″½ × 34⅛″ (70 × 86.7 cm). The Detroit Institute of Arts

Standing Female Nude, c. 1882. Black Conté crayon, 19⅛" × 13¼" (48.6 × 33.6 cm)
Courtauld Institute Galleries, London

Young Woman Powdering Herself, 1889–90. Oil on canvas, 37½″ × 31¼″ (95 × 79 cm)
Courtauld Institute Galleries, London

EIFFEL TOWER, 1889. Oil on wood, 9½″ × 6″ (24.2 × 15.2 cm)
The Fine Arts Museums, San Francisco, California. William H. Noble Bequest Fund

gesture. In composing his canvas, Seurat utilized the aesthetic protractor of Charles Henry, whose function was «to analyze all forms according to numbers and, reciprocally, to construct rhythmical forms from numbers.» This instrument, intended to measure angles and sections of the circumference, did not insure that a picture would be good, but could verify if it was harmonious or inharmonious and conclude what corrections were necessary.

More and more obsessed by the role of mathematics in art, Seurat painted *The Circus* as if he wanted to invent an algebraic formula for joy. The curve of the ring, the degree of inclination of the bodies, the ascending lines, the respective positions of persons and objects were all calculated by him at length. The gaiety of hue and value were insured by yellow, orange and red, whose intensity was heightened by the white mass of the horse. The sinuous lash of the ringmaster's whip is there to divide the scene into two areas: an area of light in the foreground, an area of shadow in the background. The rotary motion from right to left is accentuated by the direction of the somersault of the acrobat. The soaring movement and the lightness of the equestrienne (possibly Jenny O'Brien, who did trick riding in a short skirt and a ballerina's slippers, standing on her mount) are portrayed by balance within unbalance; if the orchestra conductor, above to the right, seems ready to take a fall, it is in relation to the acrobat (gyration) and the equestrienne (balanced unbalance). The triple combination is so perfect that each person has three functions: to indicate direction, contrast and rhythm.

Two innovations in *The Circus* outranked all of the others. First, in it Seurat made the statement that spectators are also actors in the spectacle. He showed them from the front (and not from the back, as in *Invitation to the Side-Show*), rising in tiers from bottom to top, and thus depicted the different classes of society. The only true spectator of the scene is the clown, in the foreground, parting the curtain; we see the equestrienne's act as he sees it. Unlike the contrabassist in *Le Chahut*, he does not play the part of a metronome; he is identified with the person looking at the picture. *The Circus* is an original attempt to introduce into a picture the viewer of the picture. Seurat had been painting his frames; now he was painting the ideal spectator and assigning him his proper place in front of his work.

The second innovation was still more extraordinary. In *The Circus*, for the first time a painter represented laughter not by persons laughing, but by Laughter itself, laughter bursting out from childish happiness. Where then is this burst of laughter? Very simply, it is the yellow zigzag to the right, that has no material significance; it is not the flash of a projector (at that time they did not exist), or lightning striking in the wings, but a luminous effect substituting for a sound effect. Seurat, with this pure symbol, this acoustical hieroglyph, painted a «yellow sound» long before Kandinsky, at the Bauhaus of Dessau, depicted sound by a straight line and translated into points a theme from the Fifth Symphony of Beethoven.

THE PAINTER AND THE MYTH

From the beginning of March 1891, Seurat, with his comrades on the arrangements committee, actively prepared for the Indépendants; every day he came to the pavilion on the Champs-Elysées in order to sort the shipments, hang up the pictures, correct their alignment and, if necessary, to lend a hand to the workmen and even to take their place. He attended the opening on March 20, and three or four days later returned to the exhibition with Angrand. Seated on a bench in the back of the room, they saw Puvis de Chavannes enter and examine, near the door, the drawings Maurice Denis had done to illustrate «Sagesse» by Verlaine. While Puvis, accompanied by a woman, slowly made a tour of the walls, Seurat said to Angrand: «He is going to notice the mistake I made in my horse.» But Puvis passed by *The Circus* without stopping, an act that hurt the young master of Chromo-Luminarism very deeply. On Wednesday March 26, once more back at the Indépendants, Seurat suffered from a very bad sore throat; he went immediately to his mother's home, where he took to bed with a fever. On Friday, he was visited at bedside by

THE CIRCUS, 1891. Oil on canvas, 73" × 59⅛" (185.5 × 152.5 cm)
Musée du Louvre, Jeu de Paume, Paris

Le Chahut (The Hullabaloo), 1889–90. Oil on canvas, 67⅛″ × 55¼″ (171.5 × 140.5 cm)
Rijksmuseum Kröller-Müller, Otterlo, Netherlands

his mistress and his newborn son, of whose existence Madame Seurat learned for the first time on this occasion. His illness, that his contemporaries described as «infectious angina» or «diphtheric influenza» (today it would probably be diagnosed as influenza complicated by meningitis) was so violent that he died on Sunday, March 29. His son, whom they had failed to isolate and quarantine, died several days later of the same illness, and his companion, pregnant with a second child, had a miscarriage.

The brutal disappearance, at the age of thirty-one years and three months, of this painter who had been «built to live a hundred years» crushed those close to him. When Van Rysselberghe burst into Verhaeren's home in Brussels on March 31, crying out: «Seurat is dead,» the latter kept repeating endlessly: «It is not possible, not possible.» And in the obituary article that the devoted to him in April, he grieved: «Seurat! Barely ten days ago, I met him at the opening of the Indépendants, facing his new canvas, *The Circus*. In my ears I hear again the sound of his voice. I recall one of his gestures, a slow, conclusive gesture that he made regularly with his hand.» Signac, overwhelmed with sorrow at the burial of his friend in the Père Lachaise cemetery, wrote to Van Rysselberghe: «Never have I seen such sadness ... Everyone was overcome. The family arranged for a superb — too superb — funeral ... Excuse the incoherence of this letter. I am addleheaded and witless.» The inventory of Seurat's works (not including the pictures that had been sold), completed on May 3 under the direction of Félix Fénéon, included 6 notebooks of sketches, 407 drawings, 163 «croquetons» and 42 canvases (the Dorra-Rewald catalogue would give the number as 65). Madame Seurat had *The Circus* hung above the bed where her son had died; she allocated half of the estate to Madeleine Knoblock, and gave a picture or a drawing to each of Seurat's friends.

The premature halt to his career was one of the great dramas in the field of painting in the nineteenth century, for the painter had not had the time to accomplish all he had set out to do. A few months before his death, he had confided in Teodor de Wyzewa that he «had in advance established an agenda for the work he wished to achieve during the next thirty years.» Charles Henry, like Seurat born in 1849, died in 1926, having become director of the laboratory on the physiology of sensations at the Sorbonne and having done some very exciting work. He initiated the law of energetics, invented irichromatin, a painting process that produced, without any solid color, «colored molecular landscapes» similar to the designs made by frost on windowpanes in the winter. One can let oneself dream for a moment about what Seurat might have done if he had lived as long a Charles Henry.

First, he would have retouched *The Circus*, that he considered to be unfinished, and added to it spectators on the steps (he had already indicated lightly, in blue, with his brush, this addition). Then he would have thrown himself into the creation of a huge canvas, about which he frequently spoke to his friends, that was to be the companion to *La Grande Jatte*; its subject was the Place Clichy. Undoubtedly the scene was to be set at nightfall, for each evening he went out to draw in the city, in the light of oil lamps. «Death surprised him when he was completely preoccupied with the Parisian night and its lighting,» said Gustave Kahn. It seems as if I can actually see that work, *A Saturday Evening, Place Clichy* (I suppose that, after evoking the pleasures of Sunday, he would have selected those of Saturday), with about forty people loitering around the statue of Marshal Moncey, that already at that time stood on the square, among the cold lights and the warm shadows.

Subsequently, he would have probably been engaged to do the decoration for some public building, like Aman-Jean, from whom were ordered some frescoes for the Sorbonne and the Marsan Pavilion. Verhaeren reflected: «If the future had been kind to him, one would certainly have seen him attempt decorative murals and perpetuate the work of Puvis de Chavannes, at the same time transforming it and perfecting it.» Seurat was the sole modern painter capable of rivaling the fresco painters of the Renaissance, and undoubtedly he would have left us a body of murals that would be compared today to the achievement of Piero della Francesca in decorating the chapel of Saint Francis in Arezzo.

HARBOR AT GRAVELINES, c. 1890. Oil on canvas, $27^{9}/_{16}'' \times 35^{7}/_{8}''$ (70 × 91 cm)
Rijksmuseum Kröller-Müller, Otterlo, Netherlands

The Channel in the Gravelines Harbor, Petit Fort-Philippe, 1890
Oil on canvas, 29" × 36¾" (73.7 × 93.5 cm)
Indianapolis Museum of Art. Gift of Mrs. James W. Fesler in memory of Daniel W. and Elizabeth C. Marmon

THE CHANNEL IN THE GRAVELINES HARBOR, ONE EVENING, 1890
Oil on canvas, 25¾″ × 32½″ (65.4 × 82 cm)
The Museum of Modern Art, New York. Gift of William A. M. Burden, donor retaining life interest

Each summer he would have executed a series of vacation pictures, no longer of the English Channel, but of the Mediterranean, and later would have gone to the countries of Africa and Scandinavia to delve deeply into the study of heat and cold in painting. He would have varied his brushstroke, as Kahn foresaw: «His evolution would have been fairly diversified, for even though he was certain that to him the *point* represented artistic verity, he might well sometimes have doubted that it was the ultimate verity.» According to Alphonse Germain, in «For Beauty» («Pour le Beau,» 1893), he would even have become more flexible concerning his theory of contrasts. «When death interrupted his task, he had just renounced *in places* the *simultaneous* contrast of tones to confine himself to their *successive* contrast.» And I imagine that in his last period, he would have combined hallucinatory and abstract painting, done experiments on the interaction of colors antedating those of Joseph Albers, who in 1963 devoted a book and serigraphs to abstract Chromo-Luminarism.

Whatever works he might have created if his too early demise had not deprived the history of art of them, Seurat will forever remain the prototype of an artist submitting to a rigorous discipline that, far from checking his creative impulses, refined them and enabled him to conquer the unknown. «I painted that way only in order to discover something new, an art exclusively mine,» he said to Signac. His passionate and rational quest for the best possible visual sensation led him to establish an order of appearances according to two principles that are the very essence of the progressive spirit: Light and Harmony.

SEASCAPE AT GRAVELINES, 1890. Oil on wood panel, 6¼″ × 9¾″ (16 × 24.5 cm)
Courtauld Institute Galleries, London

BIOGRAPHY

1859 Birth of Georges Pierre Seurat, December 2, 60 rue de Bondy in Paris. He was the third child of Antoine Seurat, former court officer of the Tribunal of the Seine at La Villette, who for three years had been living on his income.

1862 The Seurats moved into a new apartment, 110 boulevard Magenta.

1863 The family grew with the birth of a fourth child, Gabriel, who was to die at the age of five.

1869–1874 During his school years, Seurat was introduced to painting by his uncle, Paul Haumonté-Faivre, a linendraper who took him on his painting trips on Sundays.

1875 He attended drawing lessons at a night school, 17 rue des Petits Hôtels, directed by the sculptor Jules Lequien. There he became acquainted with Edmond Aman-Jean, who was to become his best friend.

1878 Having passed the examination for the Ecole des Beaux-Arts, on March 19 he became a student in the class of the painter Henri Lehmann.

1879 He rented a studio, at 32 rue de l'Arbalète, where he worked in the company of Aman-Jean and Ernest Laurent. In May, he visited the IVth Impressionist Exhibition. On November 8, he enrolled in the 119th Infantry regiment in Brest, for his one-year military service.

1880 He read David Sutter's articles on *The Phenomena of Vision* and filled a notebook with sketches. Discharged in November, he rented a studio in Paris, at 19 rue de Chabrol, where he produced his first important works.

1881 He studied Delacroix methodically. That summer, he spent two months with Aman-Jean at Pontaubert, in Burgundy.

1882 A series of drawings with Conté crayons. Began to paint *Stonebreakers.*

1883 Submitted two drawings to the Salon; the jury accepted his portrait of Aman-Jean, but not the portrait of his mother embroidering.

1884 *Bathing at Asnières*, that he prepared for the Salon, was rejected. Seurat then exhibited this picture in the show that the Group of Independent Artists opened on May 15 in a shack in the courtyard of the Tuileries. He was one of the founders, on June 4, of the « Société des Artistes Indépendants. »

1885 He regularly attented the Monday gatherings of the Naturalist writer Robert Caze, and met there all of the artistic and literay *avant-garde.* During the summer, he vacationed in Grandcamp, in Calvados. Starting in October, he applied Pointillism to *La Grande Jatte,* begun the previous year.

1886 From May 15 to June 15, *La Grande Jatte* created a sensation at the VIIIth Impressionist Exhibition (from which Degas deleted the word « Impressionist, » because Monet, Renoir and Sisley withdrew their submissions). Seurat made the acquaintance of Félix Fénéon and Charles Henry. In July and August, he stayed at Honfleur. In the fall, he worked on *The Models,* in a new studio, 128b Boulevard de Clichy.

1887 On February 2 Seurat attended the opening of the Salon of the XX in Brussels, where he exhibited *La Grande Jatte* and six seascapes. In Paris, Van Gogh invited him to his room on the Rue Lepic. Formation of the Neo-Impressionist group, with Paul Signac, Albert Dubois-Pillet, Charles Angrand, etc.

1888 In January, Seurat, together with his friends, exhibited in the offices of the « Revue indépendante, » directed by Fénéon. The Salon des Indépendants (March 22 – May 3), where he showed *The Models, Invitation to the Side-Show* and eight drawings, was very successful. In August and September, stayed at Port-en-Bessin. Van Gogh wrote from Arles to his brother Théo: « What does Seurat do? ... I have often thought about his sistem. »

1889 In February, he was once more invited to participate in the Salon des XX in Brussels; among the twelve works he showed were six seascapes of Port-en-Bessin. Beginning of his liaison with Madeleine Knoblock. In June, a sojourn at Crotoy. He moved in October and went to live in a lodging at 39 Passage of the Elysée-des-Beaux-Arts. Neither his mother nor his friends were informed of this change of address.

1890 On February 16, Seurat's son was born; the artist acknowledged paternity and named him Pierre Georges. At the Indépendants, March 20, he showed some works, including *Le Chahut*. Jules Christophe devoted to him one instalment in the series, *The Men of Today*. During the summer, Seurat stayed in Gravelines, on the North Sea.

1891 Second pregnancy of Madeleine Knoblock. On February 2, Seurat attended a banquet in honor of Symbolism and of Jean Moréas. He took part in the VIIth Salon des Indépendants, where, beginning March 20, he exhibited five of his works, including *The Circus*. On March 26,

suffering an attack of infectious angina or diphtheria, he had himself cared for at his mother's home; on the 27th, his mistress joined him there with their son. He died on March 29, at six o'clock in the morning, and his burial took place on March 31 at the Père Lachaise cemetery.

1900 Félix Fénéon organized a Seurat retrospective at « La Revue blanche. » There were 53 works listed in the catalogue, but actually it consisted of 64 paintings (including 26 « croquetons ») and 300 drawings. 10 pictures, 10 « croquetons » and 50 drawings were sold.

BIBLIOGRAPHY

GENERAL STUDIES

Jules CHRISTOPHE: *Seurat*, collection « The Men of Today, » No. 368 (Paris, Léon Vanier, 1890).

André LLHOTE: *Georges Seurat* (Rome, Valori Plastici, 1922).

Gustave COQUIOT: *Seurat* (Paris, Albin Michel, 1924).

Lucie COUSTURIER: *Seurat* (Paris, Georges Crès, 1926).

John REWALD: *Georges Seurat*, 2nd edition reviewed (New York, Wittenborn, 1946; Paris, Albin Michel, 1948).

Jacques de LAPRADE: *Seurat* (Paris, Aimery Somogy, 1951).

W. I. HOMER: *Seurat and the Science of Painting* (Cambridge, Massachusetts, The M. I. T. Press, Vol. XVIII, 1964).

John RUSSEL: *Seurat* (London, Thames and Hudson, 1965).

Roger FRY: *Seurat*, with a foreword and notes by Sir Anthony Blunt (London, Phaidon Press, 1965).

Henri PERRUCHOT: *La Vie de Seurat* (Paris, Hachette, 1966).

Pierre COURTHION: *Georges Seurat* (Paris, Editions Cercle d'Art, 1969.

Jean SUTTER: *Les Néo-impressionistes* (Lausanne, Bibliothèque des Arts, 1970).

ANALYSES OF PICTURES

D. C. RICH: *Seurat and the evolution of La Grande Jatte* (Chicago, The University of Chicago Press, 1935).

Douglas COOPERG *Georges Seurat, Une Baignade, Asnières* (London, Gallery Books, 1946).

STUDIES ON THE DRAWINGS

Les Dessins de Georges Seurat, preface by Gustave Kahn (Paris, Bernheim-Jeune, 1929).

Germain SELIGMAN: *The Drawings of Georges Seurat* (New York, Curt Valentin, 1947).

Robert L. HERBERT: *Seurat's Drawings* (New York, Shorewood, 1962; London, Studio Vista, 1965).

Joseph-Emile MULLER: *Seurat: dessins* (Paris, Fernand Hazan, 1975).

Antoine TERRASSE: *L'Univers de Seurat* (Paris, Henri Screpel, « Les Carnets de dessins, » 1977).

CATALOGUES RAISONNES

Henri DORRA and John REWALD: *Seurat, l'œuvre peint, biographie et catalogue critique* (Paris, Les Beaux-Arts, 1959).

César-Meyer de HAUKE: *Seurat et son œuvre*, 2 vol. (Paris, Gründ, 1961).

Fiorello MINERVINO: *Tout l'œuvre peint de Seurat*, introduction by André Chastel (Paris, Flammarion, 1973).

We wish to thank the owners of the pictures of Seurat reproduced herein, as well as those collectors who did not wish to have their names mentioned:

MUSEUMS

BELGIUM

Musées Royaux des Beaux-Arts de Belgique, Art Moderne, Brussels – Musée des Beaux-Arts, Tournai.

CZECHOSLOVAKIA

Prague Museum.

FRANCE

Musée du Louvre, Paris – Musées Nationaux. Bequest of Pierre Lévy.

NETHERLANDS

National Museums Vincent Van Gogh, Amsterdam – Rijksmuseum Kröller-Müller, Otterlo.

UNITED KINGDM

The Fitzwilliam Museum, Cambridge – Glasgow Museums and Art Galleries – The British Museum, London – Courtauld Institute Galleries, London – The National Gallery, London – The Tate Gallery, London.

U.S.A.

The Baltimore Museum of Art – Albright-Knox Art Gallery, Buffalo, New York – Fogg Art Museum, Cambridge, Massachusetts – The Art Institute of Chicago – The Cleveland Museum of Art – The Detroit Institute of Arts – Indianapolis Museum of Art – Nelson Gallery-Atkins Museum, Kansas City, Missouri – The Norton Simon Foundation, Los Angeles – The Minneapolis Institute of Arts – The Metropolitan Museum of Art, New York – The Museum of Modern Art, New York – The Solomon R. Guggenheim Museum, New York – Smith College Museum of Art, Northampton, Massachusetts – Museum of Art. The Rhode Island School of Design – The Saint Louis Art Museum, Missouri – The Fine Arts Museums, San Francisco – National Gallery of Art, Washington, D.C. – The Phillips Collection, Washington, D.C. – Yale University Art Gallery, New Haven, Connecticut.

GALLERIES

Stephen Hahn Gallery, New York – Sidney Janis Gallery, New York.

PRIVATE COLLECTIONS

Mr. et Mrs. Alexander Lewyt, New York – Mr. and Mrs. Paul Mellon, Upperville, Virginia.

LIST OF ILLUSTRATION

Artist's Mother (The) 20

«Baignade» (Study for Une) 22
Banks of the Seine at Suresnes 22
Barbizon Forest 19
«Bec du Hoc» (The), Grandcamp 54
Boats, Low Tide, Grandcamp 55
Bridge at Courbevoie (The) 69

Café-Concert 62
Café Singer 61
«Chahut» (Le) 87
Channel at Grandcamp (The) 50
Channel in the Gravelines Harbor (The),
    One Evening 91
Channel in the Gravelines Harbor (The),
    Petit Fort-Philippe 90
Circus (The) 86
Clown and Pony 65
Concert Européen (At the) 63

Eiffel Tower 84
End of the Jetty at Honfleur 51

Farm Laborer with Hoe 9
Fishermen 23

Gleaner (The) 8
«Grande Jatte» (The Island of La) 40
«Grande Jatte» (The Seine at La ... in the
    Spring) 48
«Grande Jatte» (Study for La ...) 32
«Grande Jatte» (Study for Sunday Afternoon
    on the Island of La ...) 45
«Grande Jatte» (Sunday Afternoon on the
    Island of La ...) .... 46—47
Grenouillère (La) 49

Harbor at Gravelines 89
House among Trees 16

Invitation to the Side-Show .... 66—67
Landscape in the Outskirts of Paris 19

Maria at Honfleur (La) 56
Men Walking in a Field 14
Models (Study for the ...) 57

Nurse (The) 43

Orange Vendor (The) 17

Peasant at Work 11
Peasants Driving Stakes 5
Peasants in the Field 15
Place de la Concorde, Winter 31
Port-en-Bessin .... 70—71
Port-en-Bessin, Entrance to the Harbor ... 73
Port-en-Bessin: The outer Harbor (High
    Tide) 75
Port-en-Bessin: The Outer Harbor (Low Tide) 72
Portrait of Edmond-François Aman-Jean .. 6

Rue Saint-Vincent, Montmartre 29

Seascape at Gravelines 92
Seascape at Port-en-Bessin, Normandy ... 74
Seated boy with Straw Hat 24
Seated Model 58
Seated Model, Back 59
Shore at Bas-Butin, Honfleur 53
Standing Female Nude 82
Steamboat (The) 68
Stonebreaker (The) 11
Stonebreakers (The) «Le Raincy» ... 12, 13
Sunday at Port-en-Bessin 76

Theatre Stage 60

View of «Le Crotoy», from Upstream ... 81

Watering Can (The) 18
Woman Fishing 39
Woman Knitting 21
Woman with the Monkey 37
Women near the Water 38

Young Girl in a «Chapeau Niniche» ... 36
Young Woman with a Drawing Pad 35
Young Woman Powdering Herself 83